High Praise for

The 5 Frequencies

of High Performance

James is so knowledgeable, and knowledge is the new currency. James will teach you, James will prepare you, and James will help create major shifts in your thinking and in your life. James Dentley has helped me so much throughout the years and now his book will help you too!

Les Brown
World's Leading Motivational Speaker

James Dentley has been my brother for over 20 years, and I know firsthand what he can do and teach. This is a powerful read that will enlighten, educate and empower everyone that truly wants to succeed.

Bill Walsh
America's Business Coach

The 5 Frequencies of High Performance

The 5 Frequencies of High Performance

The Ultimate Guide to Elevating and Accelerating Your Personal and Professional Growth

by James Dentley

Silver Torch Press

Beverly Hills, CA

The 5 Frequencies of High Performance: The Ultimate Guide to Elevating and Accelerating Your Personal and Professional Growth ©2017 by James Dentley

www.JamesDentley.com
JD@JamesDentley.com

Printed in the United States of America.

ISBN 978-1-942707-67-7
Library of Congress Control Number: 2017956301

 Published by Silver Torch Press
www.SilverTorchPress.com
Jill@SilverTorchPress.com

Dedication

I want to thank my incredible wife and best friend, Kara, for her constant love and support.

To my children, Paris and J-4, who inspire me every day and make me proud.

To my mother and three sisters, who have believed in me and supported me every day of my life!

To my friends, Milton Howard, Bill Walsh, Les Brown, and Jose Baeza. You encourage me and supported me, and I am truly thankful to you all for your love and friendship.

Table of Contents

CHAPTER ONE
Frequency

When I am speaking to a group of people—whether it be a group of ten, twenty, or twenty thousand—I hit a zone. Within seconds of opening my mouth, it's like I'm having an out-of-body experience. I go into what I call a state of flow. I tap into a higher-level frequency that is above my own understanding, and I just go with it. I don't worry about what I am going to say and how I am going to look; I worry about what I am going to give. I go into the frequency of love—a spiritual frequency that flows because I am giving of myself to so many other people. This creates synergy. As I charge myself up to my highest frequency in order to give, I open myself to them and am then able to harness the energy of everyone in the room. In this way, we touch each other and magnify the inner power we each possess.

People in my audiences tell me all the time that they don't just hear me; they can feel me. That's by design and by intention, as I have learned how to tap into the frequency that creates that experience. I am able to move into that zone very quickly because of the way I prepare my mind and my spirit beforehand. I push my energy up, and my delivery and intention are pure because it is all about giving to my audience. This is on purpose.

Twenty years ago, I gave a talk to a room of three hundred people. I made the crowd laugh, cry, think, and learn, all while inspiring them and challenging them to be better. Afterward, Larry Raskin, a mentor and great friend of mine, came up to me with tears in his eyes and said, "James, when you learn to be the same person off the stage that you are on the stage, nothing will ever stop you."

I never forgot those words. However, I didn't know what he really meant. I didn't know how to balance my life in that way. I found that on the stage I could be one thing, and I could achieve financially, but my personal or spiritual life was likely to be out of balance. Or, I would get one spiritual life in balance, and something else would fall out of balance. For instance, at one point, my health was out of balance. My financial life got out of balance as a result because I was tired and didn't feel good. I didn't take action because I didn't feel like it. My knees hurt, and I wasn't breathing properly. I had gained a lot of weight. I had sarcoidosis. This led to a victim mindset where I just went with my feelings. I made up excuses for everything that I was doing, and those excuses didn't serve me.

I remember all the times when I was at low frequency and low energy—all the times when I didn't know what to do. I self-destructed, marriages were destroyed, families fell apart, and businesses were ruined. I fell because when things went wrong, I went wrong with them.

Then I flipped a switch and made a decision that changed my life forever.

For the very first time in my life, every single thing is in balance now. Do I have challenges? Yes, they still show up, but I am able to stay in total balance in every aspect of my life in spite of them. My health is better than it has been in the last twenty years. I am able to run up and down the stairs, and I look good in my clothes again. I have an amazing relationship with the most incredible wife and best friend I could ever have. The relationships I have with my friends, my family, and my partners are all value-based relationships. These are things that make me feel good every single day because I get a chance to be part of something that's greater than myself; I get to be part of the visions of so many other people. Some of them enroll into my vision as well, and together we find synergy and create something even bigger and more powerful. The natural by-product of this kind of synergy has been greater levels of success for both me and those I am serving and being served by. When I look at my business and financial life, I am making more money and having more financial opportunities than I have ever had before.

Spiritually, I know how to stay plugged into the universe. I stay in prayer and meditation so that I am able to stay present for other people and love them without any judgment whatsoever. I live a life of expectancy, of giving and sharing, of gratitude and acceptance. I strive to live a life of humility, understanding that humility doesn't make you weak. It makes you able and strong, for in that space, you understand some battles don't have to be fought because they were never yours to fight in the first place.

I have been happy pretty much every day for the last ten years of my life. I feel as if I am one with everything in the world. I get up every morning and look at the trees, the sun, and the moving clouds. I hear the birds chirp. I notice the little things. My sense of awareness has been heightened to a level that I have never dreamt before. My mindset has expanded to what is possible and, more important, I don't look at impossibility anymore. I just look with my imagination at the things that can be created.

I am able to live in this state because I have discovered how to find that peace and gratitude on purpose, and how to stay there. I have the tools for that, and now I want to share those tools with you.

The Frequencies of Success

It is not a matter of good luck or good fortune. It is a matter of science. I am going to show you how you can apply the universal law of frequency to your life to create more power, more balance, more love, and more success than you have been able to achieve thus far. You simply have to calibrate your life in a way that you are able to tune into the exact frequency of what you're seeking. Once you can do that, you will be immersed in that frequency, and you will be sitting right in the middle of the path of all that you desire. It will naturally come to you because you are riding and elevating in the same current.

Specifically, I am going to show you how to increase your vibrations and tap into the highest frequencies of these areas of your life:

- The frequency of your spirit.
- The frequency of your mindset.
- The frequency of your physical body.
- The frequency of your relationships.
- The frequency of your financial stability.

I call these the Five Frequencies of Success. In order to play in the highest frequencies available to you, those five frequencies have to be in harmony with each other. As in all things, they are all already connected. It's comparable to the way a butterfly flaps its wings and that movement affects the atmospheric pressure around the entire world. It is like the ripple effect across a pond. When one thing moves, everything else moves. By raising one of your five frequencies, you raise another. When you invest an organized effort into raising all of them at the same time, you will experience exponential growth across all areas of your life.

The reverse is also true. When you neglect one area of frequency, there will be consequences across every facet of your life.

To illustrate this interconnectivity, imagine you are physically firing on all cylinders. You feel good, you look good, and you operate good. Now, if you continue to move forward in the other frequencies as well, you will begin to be good and you will bring good experiences to the world. However, if you 'are in great physical shape, but then you 'are a jerk to everyone you see, there's no victory in that at all. You don't win anything because you are still operating on an overall low, disruptive frequency. You get uncertainty. You go up and down in success and can't figure out why. You blame other people and go into the frequency of being a victim and living in fear. This is the lowest frequency of all and offsets the balance of everything. If you feel like you are not good enough, you will prove it. If you feel like you are not worthy of your partner, then you will destroy your relationship. If you don't feel like you can physically conquer the obstacles before you, then you will destroy your body and decide to choose death over life.

Like Attracts Like

The first principle that you need to understand, and which is the basis of everything I am going to share with you, is that frequencies will always attach themselves to like frequencies. Whatever you put out into the universe—your deposit, if you will—is going to be moving along, looking for that same frequency somewhere else that it can attach itself to. If you put out a negative frequency, it will attract a negative result or negative energy. If you put out a positive frequency, it can only attract a positive result. Every choice you make, every thought you think, every word you say—these are all deposits that you are making into the universe, and you will get a like return on that investment.

Everything is Energy

Frequency is so powerful because it is made of pure energy, which is the fabric of the universe. It is like the binary code of our existence—the ones and zeros that bring everything else into being. This quantum substance has an intelligence all its own. Years ago, there was an experiment where they focused a proton of light, aimed at a slit in a piece of paper. When the slit was closed, the proton of light changed its direction to find an opening. It changed its own trajectory. Essentially, it made a decision.

We talk about God coming into the world as light. God's light is still here today, and that light—that energy—has intelligence.

When you look back at some of the revelations of the great scholars of our time, you can see patterns. Einstein said, given the order of this universe, there is no doubt that there is a God. He is often quoted as saying, "No problem can be solved from the same level of consciousness that created it." There is some speculation over whether he is the originator of those words, but the truth still stands that if you want to rise to a higher level of living or experience in your life, you must raise the frequency at which you operate. You cannot get to a higher frequency operating on the same frequency that you are on. In order to raise up, you must go up.

Constant Motion

Even if it appears that your life is stagnant, it is not. You have to actively make the decision of where to guide your energy and your choices every moment. Many motions and decisions are invested into staying still. It's not too late to invest that energy in new ways. You can learn to operate within new frequencies, and they will give you the life that you really desire. However, you have to be willing to overcome your fear. You have to be willing to step outside of that fear and step into your possibilities.

Recognize that your life is already in motion. You are continuously shaping the information that comes into your life, and your life is continuously being shaped by the information you receive. Everything you know is based on what you were told or what you have learned because of experience. Nothing is good or bad until you give that meaning to it. This is a continuous process and people are wired with the ability to continually be learning something new.

Just imagine if, as a baby, you never learned to walk, crawl, cry out, or speak. As you got older, imagine that you never learned to read, to write, or to follow traffic laws. In your relationships, imagine if you never learned to read cues of emotion. But you did all of these things. Thus, you have a track record of learning new things throughout your life and of always being in motion. And this continues today. Nothing has changed. You are still in motion and still able to learn and apply new things.

Commit to Success

Ultimately, your journey is about first identifying that these frequencies exist and then taking the action necessary to plug into them. They have always been here. They will always be here—regardless of what you decide to do with them.

The bottom line is that winning isn't everything, but wanting to win is. Success is connected to continuous action. It is largely a matter of hanging on after everyone else lets go. You are not finished when you are defeated; you are only finished when you quit. It is about persevering over everything that comes your way and understanding that you can overcome whatever it may be by tapping into a different frequency. You are beautifully and wonderfully made. You are one of the royal priests or priestesses of the Most High. You are the infinite intelligence of this planet and have a divine right to its purest energy. When you plug into that energy, you naturally start moving in harmony with the things that give you the results you want and away from the things that give the results you fear.

You have to expect to win. Success demands that you have what it takes to take what success demands. When you fail to plan, you plan to fail, so focus on actions that produce successful results, create systems that monitor those results (positive and negative), and then make the proper adjustments. This is no different than an airplane flying to Hawaii that is blown off course many times but is brought back into alignment by a trained pilot following reliable and time-proven instruments. You have got to be committed to your commitment. You have to eliminate 'retreat' and have a maintenance plan that will keep you on track. Throughout this book, as we talk about different levels of frequency, we are going to hone in on that maintenance plan. I am going to give you a blueprint for how to get to the breakthrough, tap in to a higher level of frequency, and live there for the rest of your life.

CHAPTER TWO
Break Away to Break Through

The challenge in changing your frequency is that you have been programmed to create in a certain kind of way, and that certain kind of way is what feels natural and comfortable to you, even if it's not the best way. In his book *Beyond Miracles*, Deepak Chopra says that real life will constantly create its own reality.

For instance, if you were to put on a pair of green sunglasses right now, everything would be green. If you were raised that way, then that would be your reality. If somebody else had a pair of yellow sunglasses, their reality would be defined by a completely different color scheme than yours. That's one reason ten people can look at a picture and have ten different interpretations of what that picture is depicting.

These frequencies and paradigms are locked in from the early days of our development. Similar to a religion, these frequencies will most likely be determined by the culture and subcultures of where you live and the family in which you are raised. For instance, if you grew up in India, it's statistically likely that you will be Hindu. Similarly, you are likely to adopt the patterns and frequencies that you were raised by, and then you will go on to amplify those frequencies because that is what you, in turn, will put out into the universe. The bottom line is that our environment often determines our frequency, which then determines the frequency that we put out, which then determines what we get back.

If you want to rise to another level of experience in your life, remember that you don't get in life what you want—you get in life what you expect. You get in life who you are. For instance, I grew up in a pretty positive environment most of my life. However, it lacked the vision of possibility. Instead, we operated on a frequency that kept us safe—one that we knew would keep us comfortable where we were. It wasn't bad or good. It was okay. It was just fine. However, in order for me to imagine and to achieve possibilities, I had to break out of the status quo and set a new intention and a new frequency to my life.

In order to do that, you have to quiet your mind and thoughts to the point that you can see them as an "other" outside of yourself, instead of identifying with them as if they are you, and the only truth of the universe. If you can do that, you can go into the gap between what you think is possible and what is actually possible. If you can slide into that space, you can manifest anything. We have all been indoctrinated with stereotypes, limiting beliefs, and false truths. That's just a part of life because, again, what you live, you learn; what you learn, you practice; and what you practice, you become.

If you aren't getting what you want right now, the good news is that energy is fluid, and you have the power to reshape your makeup. You can tap into the frequency of higher achievement, of a higher level of living in your spiritual life, your physical life, your relationships, your financial life, and your mindset. Improvement in any and every area of life is accessible to everyone. It is within your reach right now.

Set Your Own Frequency

You can survive and find happiness and tranquility in any situation that you find yourself in because you will adapt. This is true even for people who are in prison. The mind finds a way to survive these things. It's your mind's job to adapt to the frequency of your environment and find a status quo. However, by the same token, you have the power to set your own frequency, regardless of your environment, and then your environment will adapt to the frequency that you've set.

This takes vision and courage.

When you decide to adjust your dial to a new frequency, you may find yourself alone at first. In order to stay in that state, you have to have the courage to be alone until your environment begins to adapt. If the right people aren't there, then you have to play there all the time until they come. You have to turn your vision inward so that you can see out through your mind's eye instead of your physical eyesight. When you can view your life through that perspective, you won't be deceived by the shadows being cast by moving light. You will have a fixed perspective, and you will be able to keep that perspective bright at all times. Nothing can be accomplished without having that vision and harmony. Even if you are all alone, if you put that harmony and frequency out into the universe, it's guaranteed to start coming back to you.

What you want always wants you.

The energy of the universe is always in a state of motion guided by attraction. These are constants in your life, and in order for you to make adjustments and stay in alignment with what you want, you also need to always be moving. It's like a dance. The sun comes up, and the sun goes down. The tide goes in, and the tide goes out. It is the yin and the yang. It is the positive and negative posts on the battery. These things work in harmony with each other.

How to Change Your Frequency

How can you engage in this dance and access a higher frequency than the one you are currently on?

The first step is to become aware that it is real and available to you. Once you learn and discover, first of all, that it is possible, then you can learn how to work in harmony with these things. This is done by relaxing and getting into those quiet moments that allow your pure genius to show up. Your unique process for this will be different than someone else's. However, you will find your way there if you desire it and ask for it. From that space, you will begin to ask yourself better questions about everything. These questions are the beginning of creation. Questions steer the creative energy of your thoughts with intention and tap in to possibility. Everything is formed from a thought, and every thought is in a constant state of vibration. Everything, down to the molecules in atoms of energy, vibrates continuously and always. The universe is in constant motion. Nothing in the world rests, and we can't rest either.

The moment you realize that is a moment when the light shines directly on you, illuminating what is possible. However, when a light shines directly on you, its brightness is enlightening, but it also leaves a shadow somewhere. Most people tend to go into the shadows, and they want to hide. They want to get away.

I went through this for many, many years. About twenty-five years ago, I felt like I had a gift. I could see and feel things, but I didn't know what they meant, so I would sabotage myself. That's what most of us do. We go into a life of self-sabotage because we don't want to take the responsibility of stepping into something that we don't understand. To illustrate this, I will share with you the story of a captured soldier.

The soldier was captured as a prisoner of war by the Vietcong. As this soldier sat in prison, every day he listened at the window and heard the firing squad say, "Ready, aim, fire!" and then the sounds of shooting. He would hear a thud hit the ground, and someone would announce that one of the prisoner's comrades was dead. This went on for days and days until finally men came to his cell, walked the soldier out to a courtyard with the firing squad and a black door, and put him against the brick wall. The lieutenant walked up to him and said, "I am going to give you the same choice I gave all of your comrades. They have all made the wrong choice. If you go through the black door on the far side of this courtyard, there are things that may destroy you, unlike anything you have ever seen. You may be eaten alive, and your brain may turn to mush. But if you face the firing squad, it is certain death. So, are you going to walk through the black door, or are you going to face the firing squad?"

The soldier replied, "Like my comrades, I want to stand up as a soldier. I believe in what I believe in, and I believe in them. I'm not sure of what's through the black door. I will face the firing squad. You can kill me now."

And so they did.

One of the sergeants walked up to the lieutenant and asked, "How come everyone always chooses to die? What's really behind that door?"

The lieutenant said, "Behind that door is actually freedom, but people would rather choose a known hell than an unknown heaven."

Most of the time, we get so afraid of things we don't understand that we make up excuses and meanings. We create meanings to protect ourselves, but it really hurts us because it starves off our possibilities. What would have happened if the Wright brothers were more consumed with the possibility of crashing off a mountain than they were with the imagined possibility of being able to fly? What would have happened if John F. Kennedy had never dared us to conquer the moon? What would have happened if Abraham Lincoln hadn't stood up and said he wanted to do something about slavery and go against the country? You can see these examples throughout history—scores of achievers and achievements that went beyond imagination.

They paved the way for the likes of all of us, and now the world is waiting for you. When you find that light illuminating your path, you have to choose to step into that burning light. You have to take action.

The second step is to take actions that will move you away from your old frequency patterns. In order to experience something new, something old must die. This takes a lot of courage. There are often a lot of fears tied to walking away. However, the bottom line is that if you want to get to a place you have never been, you have to do things you have never done.

I recently met a gentleman who has an organization named after his mother. The foundation has outreach programs for those with HIV and hepatitis. He told me the story about how he had hepatitis and how he's so passionate about making a difference for those who are still suffering. Chase Bank, one of the largest banks in our country, has donated a building to his cause. A major hospital is putting a clinic in to help further his mission. President Obama took an interest in his project and has supported his efforts in several ways.

Instead of going into the shadows in embarrassment, he chose to step into the burning light, and it paid off.

As you set your intentions toward specific frequencies, you will be drawn to them, and they will be drawn to you. However, in order to do this, you need to get your thoughts out of the way and tap in to instinct. Consider how a dog can hear the frequency of a dog whistle that humans can't hear. Animals can pick up those specific frequencies because they are operating on instinct. They aren't burdened by the additional thought loads of intellect and limiting beliefs. Similarly, when you adjust your sensors to a new frequency, you are stepping in between those gaps of what you believe is possible and what is actually possible. You are accessing instinct, governed by truth. From that place, you are going to move like the wind, and you are going to instinctively know which way to go to find what you're looking for.

To access the realm of instinct, you have to begin your journey by transcending the clutter of your mind and your programming. You have to start with your spirit.

CHAPTER THREE
The Frequency of Spirit

The frequency of your spirit is the core frequency that sends ripples through every other frequency you possess. You must keep it centered and firm in order to position all of your other frequencies for exponential success. The frequency of your spirit is where all other change is born. It is your north star.

There are so many definitions for spirit. The meaning depends on culture, religion, and many other factors. However, I don't want to deal with this definition from a religious point of view. Ultimately, spirit is about what begins in you and then expands outside of you. It is universal and nameless. When you get into harmony on a spiritual level, it doesn't matter what the spiritual level is called, whether it be meditation, whether it be Buddhism, whether it be Christianity, whether you are Hindu, or whether you are Muslim. The destination is the same. You are tapping in to a higher source outside of yourself. Even within the Buddhist tradition, when monks are chanting and tapping into a source that is within themselves, they are finding the universal frequency that is being broadcast back out into the entire world—the entire frequency of Earth and of all existence in the whole universe. In doing so, they are putting themselves into a state of harmony.

When you look at everything in our world, we are all in harmony with each other, and we are all connected to each other. We are all in line within a certain frequency by virtue of our existence. That's why the things that come up out of the ground always live stretching towards the sun. All things that grow, including each of us, feed off the energy and frequency of the same sun. This is symbolic of the universal energy that sustains all life.

The Zone

You are able to tap into and manipulate your spiritual frequency when you are in communion with the fundamental source of energy of the universe. You will access this through deep meditative thought or prayer. Even if you don't believe in any type of religion, you can access the power of meditation to induce that greater awareness and tap into that frequency. Meditation or prayer is the way to slow things down so that you can walk freely between the gap of what is and what is still possible. This is the act of centering yourself. In doing so, you become one with the world because you recognize that all things are already gathered into One.

For instance, when I'm outside I hear the birds chirp, and I see the clouds move. I can feel the breeze. I am in tune with what nature has to offer and recognize that it was put here for all of us to experience, to enjoy, to be a part of, and to care for. I see how nature cares for us in return by providing oxygen, food, water, and everything else our bodies require to live. All of these resources are by-products of other life cycles. The tree is planted as a seed, then pushes through toward the sunlight, breathing and exhaling to create the oxygen we need. Water is in a continuous cycle from ground to sky. The food we eat comes from the earth and goes into us and becomes a part of us, and then the excess goes back into the earth. We are part of an infinite number of cycles all moving along the same singular frequency of All Living.

As you recognize this and are able to tap in to this truth, you are then able to calibrate your frequency and your path against that great oneness and harness the power that has always been accessible to you, but has perhaps been out of harmony with where you set your past frequencies. You are already a conduit for this energy, but you have the power to either amplify or to stagnate its flow. When you harmonize with this Oneness and amplify its force, you enter the zone of creation. You can see that zone manifest all around you on a smaller scale already. In sports, you've seen times where the ball goes to a person and he hits it every single time or someone shoots the basketball and it always goes in. Personally, maybe you get into a state where you are typing and you don't make any mistakes, or you are speaking and you become very fluent in both speech and ideas. These are examples of states of flow.

Spiritually, you want to raise your frequency to the point where that flow emanates from your core out into the rest of your life. You don't want to just tap into it when you are in a meditative state, or during select activities. You want your life to be governed by that state of flow, regardless of what you're doing. When you start to inhabit that space, you begin to live your rhetoric. You understand that your faith has behavior and that that which you believe in shows up in your daily actions. You live that way. Then, the laws of attraction come into play because what you want and who you truly are will always identify themselves with each other to the point that what you want will start showing up. It has to because who you are and what you want are on the same frequency. You will naturally attract the things that you want because they will want you in return.

When you are able to tap into a spiritual frequency of that magnitude, the forces of individuals outside of you are unable to take that away from you. If they do, it is only for a moment. It is like a Weeble. They wobble, but they don't fall down. It is about making a home "in the zone." You start and end every day in peace. Even if you make some detours in between, you always know the way home.

The Power of Stories

In that sense, you begin to go on a journey to find a sense of purpose and of identifying exactly who you are. You are able to change your story. You walk through the muck and your perspective can't be changed. It's like the tale of two men Victor Frankl cites in his book, *Man's Search for Meaning.* "Two men gazed through prison bars. One saw the mud, the other the stars." Both men are in prison, but individually they are in two very different stories. It is the same with us. The stories we perceive that we are in shape our entire perspective.

Consider a woman who says, "My heart is broken." In reality, we know that if her heart was broken, she would be dead. Her heart is not broken. Something happened, and she reacted to that something by crafting a story around its meaning. Nothing is good or bad until you give that meaning to it. That meaning defines the frequency of the story you're telling yourself. Frequency will always attach itself to some story or some reason why you are feeling or acting a certain way. There's always going to be a story. If your heart is broken, that means you are tapping into that frequency and tuning into the sound of heartache. You tune into that channel that is telling the story of heartbreak.

When you tune into a channel, there are a lot of elements there. There is music, scenery, costumes, and actors. All of those things play out in your life on any frequency you can tune into—the good or the bad. What you need to recognize is that you are in control of the dial. You are the author of your stories. You have the power to shift the frequencies and to change the stories. If you have been on a lower spiritual frequency, perpetuated by the negative stories you've been telling and retelling in your life, it's not too late to change your story. You always have an opportunity to shift your perspective and start looking at the stars.

When you do, you will begin to see differently. Your expectations will begin to be different when you operate on a higher spiritual frequency. You will walk up to people and speak with a smile on your face. You will begin to hold the door for people. You will become more conscious of your fellow human beings. You will begin to be more gracious toward your team, and more understanding toward each individual. You never reach perfection, but you love even though you know there will never, ever be perfection—in you or those around you. However, you become more understanding of others' imperfections, and you become apologetic when you personally have a transgression. You own it. You are able to live an integrative life between the ideal and the reality because even in the midst of mistakes and human frailties, you are able to tap into the highest spiritual frequency, which is love. The core of that love is peace, and the core of peace is gratitude and acceptance. You take on the view of *The world is okay, and I am okay in it.*

Constant Frequencies

When you have a high level of spiritual frequency, you are able to have the ability to see and to feel with your whole experience—not just your eyes or your heart. You see with your nervous system. You can feel certain things. It is so real that if you are in a crowded mall and there is someone across the mall staring at you, on many occasions you can feel that energy being broadcast toward you. Or perhaps you've experienced a time when you started to think about someone, and then that same person "mysteriously" called you. What really happened is that the two of you crossed frequency-paths. When that happens, the two frequencies collide, and there is a natural response (hence the phone call).

These frequencies are constantly available to you, whether or not you choose to cross them or access them. I remember John Aswall once asked the question, "Do you hear music in the room?" The whole room was silent, and no one knew the right answer.

Some people wanted to be right so they said, "Yes" anyway, even though they didn't really hear music. He then asked, "Is there music in the room?" Some people said, "No, not right now." (No one knew where he was going with this.) He then said, "If I were to bring in a radio and plug it in, lift the antennas and tune it to a station, would I then begin to pick up the frequencies that are already in this room?" Everyone had an aha moment. He was demonstrating to us that, yes, there is music in the room. It's always in the room, even when we can't hear it. However, whether or not we hear it is up to us.

Mr. Doubt

Not everyone taps into this state of flow. It is not because of an incapability, but some are less aware than others as to the potential and purpose of Spirit. Your interpretation of what that means to you will be based upon where you tap into it. That's why you have certain organizations that may be more radical and more dangerous than others. One person can take the same dream as another, and the two individuals can have two different meanings of what it is based upon the frequency each person is tapped into. The energy that is set in Spirit is the energy that determines what gets done and what doesn't get done on the outside.

However, most people operate from a base of fear, and that fear is what holds you back because in that frequency you are unsure. That low frequency is the home of the serial killer called Mr. Doubt. You have to be on the lookout for Mr. Doubt because he will slay your dreams, opportunities, and possibilities from your life. It brings about procrastination, and then you live as the poem goes:

The story of a man who would figure and plan
of all the things that he intended to do,
yet when the time came for him to get in the game,
he never put anything through.

He dreamed with a smile of the after a while,
of all of the things he would do pretty soon.
He was alright at heart, but he never would start.
He could never quite get into tune.
Yet if he had done all things he had begun,
he would have lifted among those of faith.
But he was of no use, so he did not produce.
His intentions were not to win the game.
It is easy to dream, to plan and to scheme
and then let dreams drop out of sight,
but only the ones who put through with their dreams
will be the ones who will win the fight.

~ James Dentley

The Seed of Creation

So, you see that it is imperative that you don't let fear crowd out your dreams. When you live from a spiritual frequency, you ensure that your dreams keep a strong heartbeat because all dreams are Spirit waiting to take form. They are housed in your imagination as a picture, or an image of a desired future. Once you graduate from fear and are able to live from the higher frequency of Spirit, you are able to get clarity on what life really means for you and how you want it to manifest. You are then positioned to be an effective and intentional creator of every aspect of your life.

Everything you can ever want and everything you want to accomplish is already contained within you as a seed, and the makeup of that seed is Spirit. As with any seed, this seed is set for transformation. Think of a tree. The reality of the tree is housed in the reality of the seed because everything the tree is, is contained in the seed. Likewise, everything you desire is contained in the seed of your spirit. The moment you dream a desire, the entirety of the fulfillment of that dream is contained within the initial dream state, just like the tree in the seed. It is the form of the dream that precedes manifestation. Once the dream is born in Spirit, it begins to broadcast frequencies that trigger its manifestation. These manifestations are a result of a series of transformations, the first being the birth of the dream in spirit.

Imagination

Inspiration and imagination are the keys that drive any and all creation. Nothing can be seen or exist without first being created in the unseen, or the Spirit. Everything you see starts in the unseen. This is a powerful notion. In many ways, Spirit does not exist without you and is creating what's imagined. The results that stem from imagination are proof of Spirit. The spirit of what you want comes into existence the minute you want something. This inspiration, like a biofeedback loop, communicates back to you the instructions for accomplishment. Imagination and inspiration are like twins. Your imagination sparks a dream, and inspiration gives it life. "I want" begins in the imagination, and then leads to the inspired "I will." So, life begins with the "I want" of your imagination.

I – Mage

The root word of imagination is image. All images must start with yourself in mind. This is not a selfish notion, but the notion that is the root of all that is created. The root of "image" is "mage," which comes from the word "magi," meaning king. One derivative of the word magi is magic. To bring something into the realm of what can be seen is essentially true magic. Here is why the word magi or king is important.

Generally, under a monarchy where a king rules, when the king has an idea, or i-dea, meaning "I see", he has to trust enough in his idea to announce it to those who will carry out the development of his idea. Soon after, the king's idea is then rendered into existence by a body of those who actively agree. In a great sense, this is true magic. But notice again that the fruition of that magic involves those who agree with the king's idea and who play various roles in bringing the kings idea into physical reality. So, the magic happens by way of the idea first being created, and then being carried out by those who agree with and then act on that idea.

No magic happens without "I."

Everything starts by imagination and inspiration, or in-spirit, and then moves from spirit into existence. Another definition for Spirit is that which doesn't exist in physicality, but has been decided in spirit and is well on its way to fruition. But everything has to start with "I." There can be no magic without you.

The magic here, like a frequency, can easily be transferred to others for action. It is necessary to exchange with others in order to create your dream, which we will explore more as we discuss the frequency of relationships in later chapters. But first, your spirit must be solid. It is the home where you let your imagination run wild. Your image becomes a frequency that is broadcast to others and will be mirrored back to you by those in harmony with your vision. You have to broadcast the proper picture of your exact desire. This picture is another component of Spirit.

The concept of Spirit is very simple. It is an entity that resides in you as the basis for inspiration and imagination, and it is also who you are as you value the ideas that come to and from your mind. Every idea that comes to mind intends to be shared with the world. You are the one who wields the power to determine whether it will materialize beyond thought. It is through Spirit that the world transforms itself into greater existences, both on the largest scale of all humanity and within the microcosm of the world you alone create. You are the creator of your world, and a cog in the one at large. Without your spirit being set to the frequency of creation, things do not move from the unseen into what can be seen and experienced by yourself and others.

The Importance of Value

To start, you must respect your imagination by valuing what you think. The "I" creates "Magic" when the "I" is properly valued. Creating value is about confidence and trust in yourself. Lack of trust in yourself equals lack of value. A king who doubts himself can hardly expect for others to follow his ideals. So, value is established in your ability to stay aware and lend credibility to your inspirations. This inner frequency then extends beyond you, influencing others to line up with your values. Once you, like a king or magi, set the right relationships around you, your idea becomes emanate. Then, just like magic, things get done.

It all comes back to value. The amount of value you place on something is the measure of your power to transform it. It is only what you value that can be transformed. It is only what you value that can become a nourished seed.

No matter how great your idea is, or how great the imagination you may have, it cannot be exchanged without a price. Spirit is about knowing yourself and having knowledge of your value. This is important. Many times, we do not stop long enough to place a value on what we want, which will guarantee that we never make the necessary exchanges in order to receive it. It is the exchange of information that creates the basis for transformation. Imagine walking into any retail outlet and finding there aren't prices on anything. Then what? There would be no basis for exchange.

What do I mean?

Consider it this way: Gold is free. Silver is free. Diamonds are free. Vegetables are free. Beans are free. All of these things come from the ground, so in essence, they hold the same value. However, when it comes to exchange with any of those items, all of a sudden, they are valued very differently. These higher values are determined by an agreement. The person unearths the commodity and then sets a price. When making the exchange, if the person receiving the commodities agrees to the price, then value is now assessed. The actual value is not a physical entity or a physical reality. Value is completely spiritual. Value is an agreed upon entity. What I'm saying is that the true power of your Spirit cannot exist without you first placing a value on yourself. This then becomes the basis of how people approach you and treat you. They have the option to come into agreement of your terms of exchange, which is the standard of your frequency. Those who are in harmony with the frequency you set will be attracted to you. Those who are at a higher or lower frequency will pass by. The wrong person cannot stand to be in the right environment. Likewise, the right person cannot stand to be in the wrong environment.

The value of your Spirit is the price you have personally set, and agreement is the beginning of the manifestation of what you want or desire. (We will talk more about agreement in Chapter Ten.)

So, how much do you value yourself and what you want? This is not only a question that must be answered, but it must be kept at the forefront of your thinking at all times. Despite what Spirit says, if you do not know your value, you will line up with how other people value you. What you imagine to be, must be, and you cannot allow it to be reduced by what others think. Otherwise, you will end up paying yourself into an emotional debt. Do not let their sense of value transform your life. You can't develop from someone else's seed. That is a sure formula for poverty, and anyone living his or her life practicing poverty on a daily basis experiences consistently diminished results.

The energy that is set in Spirit is the energy that determines what gets done and what doesn't get done on the outside. You are a starting point. Like a seed, you are the beginning of innovative ideas. In order to ensure you are conceiving thoughts and ideas that will serve your highest purposes, it's important to align with the highest spiritual frequency possible. In order to raise your frequency to the spiritual frequency that allows you to be a conscious creator of your life, you need to be in a constant state of intentional learning, growing, and becoming.

Always Learning

I started martial arts trainings when I was 14, and I stayed in for 13 years. I trained in the Japanese style, where you start with a white belt, which means the beginning. As you move through the ranks and go through a series of exercises and accomplishments, you earn your yellow belt, then your green belt, and then on through a series of other belts until you get to the black belt. There are several degrees of black belts in martial arts. After you go through all of those, you graduate to a red and then white belt. Finally, as a grand master, you go back to a white belt; it is just a little bit thicker than the first. That white belt means that you are back at the beginning.

You are always in harmony with the universe. You are never completed. You are always learning. In life, on a spiritual level and every other level, you need to continue to learn, earn, and yearn. You want to continue to earn, and not just earn on a monetary level, but earn in your spiritual life as well, so that there can always be peace in the earnings of the other areas of your life. That kind of peace comes with a quiet intensity. When you find that sense of peace, it just resonates inside of your being, right there in your gut. It sits there and it is powerful, but it is able to sit quietly. In that state, you can find gratitude and acceptance in the fact that you don't have to run the world today. Everything doesn't have to be perfect in order for you to be happy in this moment. You can't control the world, but you can control the state you choose to be in, which makes your personal world perfect and harmonious. And when you find yourself out of balance (which you absolutely will from time to time), you will know how to go back into balance.

You will wobble, but never fall.

CHAPTER FOUR
The Frequency of Mindset

When I look back on my life, I can see and measure the stumbling blocks I have experienced. These were the times I wobbled and fell flat on my face, but then got back up again; or the times I was afraid but kept going anyway. My ability to push through the fear and the doubt and the obstacles has defined my career and, I would argue, is the only difference between me and the person who is still sitting in his cubicle dreaming of a better way. The energy required to move from dreaming to doing lies in the power of your mindset. The frequency of your mindset manifests itself in the actions that you are willing to take.

Everything in life happens twice. First the thought, and then the experience or action. The inner and then the outer, the mental and then the physical. Repeated thoughts influence your words. Repeated words influence your actions. Repeated actions influence your habits. Repeated habits define your results and who you become. People define you by what you do, and your character equals your destiny.

Early in my career, I was going through the motions, but I sometimes struggled with the belief in the inevitable outcome because I didn't yet have the knowledge and understanding that comes from the experience of arriving. However, when I began to spend time around thought leaders like John Assaraf, Bob Proctor, and others, and I became familiar with Napoleon Hill through his book *Think and Grow Rich*, I began learning about frequencies, moving energy, and the fact that we can manifest anything that we want in our lives through our thoughts and imagination. I thought of this common proverb:

> Plant a thought and reap a word;
> plant a word and reap an action;
> plant an action and reap a habit;
> plant a habit and reap a character;
> plant a character and reap a destiny.

I began to study these principles. I wondered, *What if this is true?* When the thought leaders I admired told their stories, they were not all glitter and gold. They were filled with controversy and challenges, and it seemed to be a miracle that they were standing where they were that day. It gave me hope. I went on a journey of self-discovery to find out what life was really all about. I wanted to find those quiet gaps that I could move in to—those spots of energy that I could access and tap in to that would allow me to be at rest and look at things differently.

Before that, there was a time when I wanted to commit suicide because I didn't know what the meaning of my life was. I didn't know why I was here. I thought, *Is this all life has to offer me?* I am thankful I didn't do it or even attempt to do it. However, I also recognize that I contemplated that path because my life was empty. There is a frequency to that, and I was reflecting that frequency in my life. It wasn't literally empty, any more than it is now. The problem was that my mindset was so narrow that it didn't take in the horizon. It was turned toward a brick wall and just focused on the things I perceived I couldn't control. I was resting at a low frequency.

Low Frequency Mindset vs. High Frequency Mindset

Everything begins with the way that you choose to think and the frequencies of those thoughts, which in turn creates your paradigms. Your paradigms are the way you see the world and your place in it. They are what bring meaning to all things in your life and all the experiences that you have. Most of your paradigms are learned or modeled. They are first shaped by the experiences you have as a child, but more important, how you interpreted those experiences and how you responded to them.

This truth is so important: It is never so much about what happens as it is how you respond to what happens.

Newton's Third Law of Physics tells us that for every action, there is an opposite and equal reaction. So, when something happens, what do you do to balance out that action? What do you do to break even and bring things back to equilibrium? When your mindset, or your state of being or thinking, is threatened, you will naturally go to a frequency to protect yourself because that's what the mind does when it feels threatened or experiences trauma. However, the specific frequency you go to will determine whether you eliminate the threat completely or hurt yourself even worse than the perceived threat could have.

As human beings, we are not like animals. We are not like a tiger that can bite a head off or take one swipe with its mighty claw and eliminate a threat. We are not like a monkey or gorilla with power beyond its size. We are not like a mouse that can burrow away for safety. What we do have is the ability to raise above the threat and find a solution, or we can retreat to a lower frequency where we have the ability to shut out, shut down, and shut off in response to threats. When we shrink into a lower frequency, we mute our power to solve the problem instead of magnifying our power to do so.

Consider people who are trapped in destructive cycles of addiction. In AA meetings, addicts and alcoholics talk about triggers in the form of experiences, people, places, and things. The triggers are triggers because the addict has associated frequencies with them. They become doorways for the addict to mentally walk through to get into a certain state of low frequency—often one of fear, shame, or uncertainty. If a person is out of alignment and emotionally clogged, they will respond differently to that environment than someone who isn't. Those experiences, people, places, and things may be immoveable on the timeline of your life, but how you interpret them is fluid. The frequency that you mentally and emotionally assign to those things is not static, but can and must be changed.

The frequency of your mindset has the power to trap you, or to deliver you. Your life is driven by the frequency of your predominant thoughts. When you go into experiences, you take yourself into those experiences, and either you influence them or those experiences influence you. You either act, or you are acted upon. You are a sheep, or you are a lion. Sheep are people with a low frequency mindset. These are people who whine and complain because they are a victim of circumstance. They wait for the energy of the herd to direct them where to go, instead of taking the initiative to carve out their own path.

Compare that to a lion who walks where he wants to walk, leading the way for others to follow. This is a fitting metaphor for those on a high frequency mindset. People at that level don't wait for the herd to push them. They have a singular focus on where they want to be, and they make it happen. Their gaze is steady on the outcome they want, and everything else in between is just something to step over, step around, or a tool to get them there. There are no walls. There are only opportunities. Whatever they have to go through is just something else to grow through.

However you're using your mindset right now, you are likely acting out what you perceive to be "the best way," or "the right way," or "the only way" as shaped by your current mindset and paradigms. This is why it is so important to revisit your paradigms from time to time and see how they are serving you. Even if you're operating at the highest frequency you are aware of, it does not mean you are operating at the highest frequency.

The Four Stages of Learning

Recognizing there are more frequencies beyond your current energy level brings awareness, which is the first step toward moving into a better space. When you grasp that there are a limitless number of frequencies, this will reveal to you a life without boundaries that is full of purpose. You will be able to tap in to the frequency of living above the line. When you can tap in to that, you find that you are motivated at the start of every single day. You are excited for every morning to arrive. You are excited for every night when you get a chance to lay down because you know when you wake up the next day, there is something more for you to discover, to do, and to be. You will not have to push yourself toward your future. It will be so clear in your mind that it will pull you.

Getting from here to there is a process. As in all things, you have to move through each of the four stages of learning: unconscious incompetence, conscious incompetence, conscious competence, and unconscious competence.

The first stage of learning is unconscious incompetence, which is where you don't know what you don't know. Now, that is where possibility lies. It is like with a baby. He is put in the car, and when he gets out he has just magically arrived at Grandma's house. "Things happen or don't happen, and you have no idea why. You are just along for the ride, with seemingly no control over the outcome. Your fear and your baggage are in a reciprocal feeding relationship with each other.

Then you move into the second stage of learning, which is conscious incompetence. When you move into that realm, you can make the choice to get better, to quit what you are doing, or to just stay where you are and endure it and make excuses for yourself by blaming other people for your circumstances.

Then you move into the third stage of learning called conscious competence. This is where you know how to navigate through life, but you are still not totally in control. You are not the one in control of complete expression.

Finally, you move into the fourth stage of learning, which is unconscious competence. There, you are in complete control. You recognize all of your choices and resources, and you can manipulate them for the specific outcomes you desire.

Consider these four stages of learning as they apply to learning to drive a stick-shift car. When you are operating the car for the first time, you are usually unconsciously incompetent. You don't know what you don't know. You can't find and grind it. As you get a little better at it and you realize you want to keep this car, you move into conscious incompetence, which means that now you are trying to drive forward and it is going backwards. You know you have some things to learn. If you are going to keep this vehicle, you have to learn how to do it. Then you move into conscious competence, which is where you can drive the vehicle, but it is still mechanical. You have to think about the brake, the clutch, the gas, and the shifting. Every single action is an extension of a specific thought. The movements do not come naturally. Finally, you move into unconscious competence, which is when you are driving down the road with one knee, putting on lipstick, holding a coffee, sipping the coffee, and handing your child something in the back seat (moms do this so well). Or, you are driving down the road without paying attention to where you are or where you're going, but you still manage to stay within the lines and arrive at your destination. You have done it for so long that you get into that zone and do it automatically. That's the sweet spot.

You have experienced all of these frequencies in different capacities throughout your life. You are already fluent in them. Now you can recognize them and strategically and intentionally apply them to your life for high achievement.

Reframe Your Stories

As you open your mind to intentionally move quickly through the four stages of learning, you will be transformed. Mindset is everything because it dictates how you are going to act and react in life. When you are consciously competent in your mindset, you will adopt the philosophy that when things go wrong, you don't have to go wrong with them. When things go crazy, you don't go crazy. You are able to calm down and determine what is going to be the next best thing in any situation. You will be able to look at the stories that have been running your life and rewrite the stories that aren't serving you.

When I was mentoring my clients as a life and business coach, I worked with a young lady who carried a resentment towards her mother and father because they weren't there for her while she was growing up. Resentment is intertwined with feelings of loss of control, a lack or loss of love, or not feeling good enough. It is locked in fear, which is the lowest frequency of all. In order for her to go there, she had to lower herself to that frequency. She used a story to travel there, as stories create familiar paths for us. Every story has a frequency, and every frequency will seek out a story to attach itself to—some reason why you are feeling the way you do, or why you are in the state you are in, or why you are operating the way you are. You believe that if you have a story, you have a valid reason. If you have a valid reason, you're not crazy or lazy—you're just suffering through a story line you can't control.

In the case of this young lady, her story went something like this: Her dad wasn't there because he died when she was two years old. Her mother wasn't there because she had to work two and a half jobs to support the family. As this young woman was growing up, she harbored that resentment, and it became deeply embedded into her perception of the world and her place in it. She didn't let it go, and it couldn't let go of her either because she never dealt with it. That story was running her life without her even realizing it. She was unconsciously incompetent. She took up residence at that low frequency, which crippled her ability to thrive in the other areas of her life. I first had to teach her how to reframe her story and to shift her mindset. Once she did, she was free to move her mindset into a higher frequency, and everything else in her life came into harmony.

You must always remember that if there's a story, then you wrote it. I do not say this to cast blame or to shame you. I say this so that you can realize that as you have the power to create these stories, you also have the power to rewrite them, to shift them, and to change them. Being unconsciously incompetent or unconsciously competent is not a measure of "fault." It is a measure of how fully you are applying your powers of creation to your life. When you change the way you look at things, the things you look at change.

Responsibility

You are the only person responsible for your mindset and the stories you travel through. You have a responsibility to yourself, to your family, to your community, and to the world. This is not a responsibility *for* anyone else, but it is a responsibility *to* everyone else. If you want the world to be better, you start by making your own world better. You start with you. You raise your frequency by moving into the spaces that have higher frequencies. In order to tap in to the mindset of high achievers, study high achievers so you can model them. Where they are living? Where are they spending their time? What are they reading? What is their attitude? How do they react to challenges? As you train your focus on answering these questions, your mind will become steeped in these new ways of doing things. What you focus on is where your head goes, and where the head goes, the body will follow. Remember, every action you take happens twice—first in the mind, then with the body.

As you make this shift, you draw on the true power of focus. Anything is possible when you are focused on the pathway there. When you focus on what you want to achieve, you will be hungry for more answers to even more questions. This will pull you into spaces with even higher frequencies. You will find yourself surrounded by high achievers, and you will mirror them. Your mindset will continue to shift and you will begin to make better decisions in life because you will be a lion forging your own path. You will be able to see things with absolute clarity. You will know what you want, who you are, where you are, and where you want to go. In other words, you will be crystal clear on both your why and your purpose.

CHAPTER FIVE
A Driven Mind

Most people get caught up in the how, and when they don't have an answer for that, they give up. That's looking at the situation all wrong. If you want to achieve a certain aspect or level of success in your life and live on a certain frequency, don't get caught up on the how. Get caught up in the *why*. Why do you want to get there in the first place? Once you have answered that, the how takes care of itself.

Think of a baby who sees something on the kitchen counter that he wants to get a hold of. Without ever having watched a home builders' television show or having any concept of carpentry, he will begin to construct a ladder or devise some other means to get to where he wants to go. When you have a big why, the how won't matter anymore.

A while back, I wasn't able to show up in my life at a high frequency because of the state of my physical frequency. I was afraid that any day I could have a heart attack or stroke. I had to have multiple surgeries. My sarcoidosis was killing me. My weight was killing me. I had heard about a gentleman who had gained so much weight that when he bent over to tie his shoes, it cut off his oxygen and he dropped dead on the spot. With all of these issues, I was living my life in fear, which brought everything to an even lower frequency. My spirit, my mindset, my body, my relationships, my ability to show up in my career—everything was being affected. I was clogged across the board.

I learned very quickly that a person with wealth may want many things, but a person without health wants only one. However, it wasn't until I really articulated my why that I was able to start that new path and initiate a new path of memory for my body to follow. After years of physical suffering, I decided to take my health much more seriously, and I made major life changes that had previously eluded me. What was my why?

My first wife died from cancer in her forties, and I had a young daughter and a son who needed me. There were other family members, too—siblings and a mother—who wanted me to stay around, and whom I wanted to stay around for. I didn't just want to stick around by breathing, but I wanted to continue to be a contributor in those relationships in every area possible.

When I found my why, I was able to recalibrate my mindset and the rest followed.

What is your why? Why do you really want to achieve your dreams? Why do you want to live a certain way? Are you tired of living in a low frequency existence where you don't feel good every single day? Do you want to increase the quality of your life so that you can get more out of your relationships? Do you want to give back to the planet?

Your why must be designed and not left to scattered notions of expectation. We are the only species on the planet that makes a constant decision *not* to live at its fullest capacity. A tree doesn't grow so far and then say, "I am tired of growing. I don't want to grow any taller than these four feet." No. Just like the heart's job is to beat because that's what it does, the tree will stretch towards the heavens as high as possible and extend its roots as deep into the earth as they will go because that is what it was designed to do. That growth is the *why* of its existence. Your mind hungers for this kind of singular focus so that you can fill the true purpose of your creation. Once you set your intention by defining your why, your transformation will occur without you having to make the constant decision to move. It will unravel before you like a tree unraveling from its seed. Remember, frequencies are exacting in nature. The moment you set your destiny, the frequencies of that destiny are set in stone.

Look at what mankind has done with this kind of singular focus. There are scores of achievers who have overcome their physical challenges and become successful in spite of them. Wilma Rudolph was in a wheelchair, and they said she would never walk again. Then she stood up and won a gold medal. Helen Keller was deaf and dumb. She broke through her silent prison to be a true voice in the world. People like this have latched on to their why and allowed it to move their mindset into a space of high frequency. They live life for its experience because they know that finishing and completing is happiness. Thriving and growing is happiness. Stagnation is low frequency, and that's where you get into trouble.

When you are clear on your why, you won't get distracted by the challenges that will inevitably come. Someone once said, "It is not the blowing of the wind, but it is the set of the sail because the wind blows on its own." We all will have challenges in life. In order to keep those challenges from pushing you off course, you need to have the exact coordinates of where you're going and why you're going there. It's not enough to know where. If your reason for sailing is weak, then the first big wave will be enough to make you change your mind about the journey. Instead, you have to be sold on something that's real.

Every human, in order to function properly, must also have a purpose or a set destination. Your purpose stems from your greatest desires. What do you want in life? Once this is figured out, a destiny is set. Once you set the frequency of your why and your purpose, you have a standard by which you can constantly recalibrate your direction. You will know if you're on track because you have identified the track you want to be on. This is the key to maintaining optimum frequencies.

Vision

Once you have identified your why and your purpose, you will then create your vision, which is fueled by your dreams. Dreams and visions are things that have you. In order to move into that space, you must first adjust the frequency of your mindset so that you are able to believe that you can create something that isn't there.

Consider little Johnny, who sat in his third-grade art class drawing a picture. The teacher is walking through the class, looking over kids' shoulders and smiling and giving encouragement. When she gets to Johnny, she smiles and looks down at his paper. "What are you drawing, Johnny?"

"I am drawing a picture of God," he says.

"But Johnny, nobody knows what God looks like." Johnny doesn't even look up but says, "They will in a minute."

Johnny had a vision in his mind that he didn't question. His imagination handed him a finished picture that he was going to recreate. He dared to go there. Likewise, you need to have that same courage to be a pioneer and an inventor. Maybe you're not creating something that has never existed, but maybe it has never existed in *your* life. It is the same thing, and it takes the same courage and certainty. Look around yourself right now. Whatever it is that you see around you—whether it be a TV, a chair, a rug, a comforter, a table—was first created by thought. Someone first had to identify a problem, then *decide* that he or she was going to solve that problem.

There's a story of two young men that were working in the orange groves in Florida in the hot sun. Every day, they'd journey home over a large hill. One day, they had worked extra hours and were exhausted. They only made it to the top of the hill where there was a large tree offering shade. They sat under the tree, and then they both fell asleep. One of the friends woke up first and shook his companion, saying, "Wake up! I had the most incredible dream."

"What did you dream about," asked his friend.

"I dreamt I had one thousand orange groves!"

His friend looked at him with wide eyes and said, "Wow, one thousand orange groves? If you had one thousand orange groves, would you give me half of them?"

"No way, I would not give you half of my groves."

His friend tried a different approach. "Well, then, with one thousand orange groves, would you give me one hundred groves? That is only 10 percent."

"No, I would not give you one hundred of my orange groves."

Exasperated, the friend asked, "Would you give me one orange grove?"

"No, I would not give you even one orange."

His friend looked at him in disbelief and said, "We have been friends all of our lives. How can you be this selfish? Why wouldn't you give me an orange?"

"Because you are too lazy to dream for yourself."

Remember to grab your own dream. You have to have a dream on the inside to starve off the nightmares that can be perceived on the outside. Remember the words of the poet, Larry Chengges:

Follow your dream
wherever it leads,
don't be distracted
by less worthy needs.

Shelter it, nourish it,
help it to grow -
Let your heart hold it
down deep where dreams go.

Follow your dream
pursue it with haste;
Life is too precious,
too fleeting to waste ...

Be faithful, be loyal,
then all your life through
the dream that you follow
will keep coming true.

Commitment

Armed with your why, your purpose, your vision, and your dreams, now you are ready to begin the process of going in the direction of what you want. You must maintain your commitment to stay the course. A high frequency mindset will fuel your commitment, and keeping that commitment will ensure you stay in that space of high frequency. They go hand in hand. Commitment by my definition is doing the things you said you would do after the failure has passed you. Commitment for people on a low frequency means they *have* to. But for people who operate on a high frequency, it means they *get* to. They say, "I am committed to achieving my goal. The goal is already done because I said it was done. It's already been decided." Once you make that shift and tap in to that station— the frequency of achievement—then your mind is going to take you there because you will figure it out. You will go over, under, or above; and if you don't make it to the top of the mountain, you will die on the side because all you know is that you are going this way. The decision has been made, and there is no other decision to make.

There is nothing more powerful than a made-up mind.

Mohammad Ali said it best when he said, "Champions aren't made in gyms. Champions are made from something they have deep inside them—a desire, a dream, a vision. They have to have the skill, and the will. But the will must be stronger than the skill." When you have the will, you have the fortitude to wake up every day and work on the skill. You can swallow the mistakes that come with practice. You will understand that in order to be a champion prize fighter, you can't bail every time you get hit in the face. Getting hit is just par for the course. Being on a high frequency doesn't mean trouble can't find you. Trouble will find you because these frequencies all run in harmony next to each other. Sometimes they are bound to cross paths. However, when that time comes, you don't let trouble move in. You stay committed to learning, to growing, to reading, and to studying—always reaching for those higher frequencies. You stay committed to the things you say you want to do, even if it means that sometimes you have to change your course to stay the course.

Course Corrections

There will inevitably be times when you need to make some course corrections. Don't be discouraged by this. I have a friend who says that there are times when quitting can be euphoric. That's because there are times that you are beating your head against a wall trying to make something happen for the sake of your commitment, but the wall isn't going to move because you're supposed to be walking through a door instead. It's important to stay focused on your purpose, but sometimes you need to let the Universe be creative in the way it will lead you there.

You see this with inventors all the time. Look at Post-It Notes. This company makes hundreds of millions of dollars selling their product. Did you know the Post-It Note was a mistake? The company was actually trying to make a glue that would stick better than any other glue. The end product was a glue that barely stuck at all! Did they throw it away and start over? No. They made a shift. If they had decided to throw that mistake in the garbage and try again, they would have missed an opportunity of a life time. Instead, they were able to recognize a door when they saw one.

This is also true in your life. Sometimes your mind is so made up on where you are going, and how you have to get there, that it's hard to see necessary detours for what they are—necessary detours. Remember, a detour is there to save you time and route you around a construction zone, a broken bridge, a traffic jam, or some other obstacle that is barring your way. When you come across those detours, be grateful they were given to you. If you fail to see them for what they are, they are more likely to derail you from your destination all together.

The detours that you call challenges build muscle. They make you stronger and prepare you to face even bigger challenges in the future. If you have never gone through anything, you can't get through anything. Once your mindset matures to the point that you see the things you go through as just something else to grow through, you will be unstoppable. The things that used to bother you, cripple you, stagnate you, or stop you—now they will feed you.

Don't let circumstances or detours move your mindset into a lower frequency. Make a conscious choice every day, sometimes several times a day, to stay tuned in at all times. Decide, "This is where I am going, and no one is going to stop me." When you can do this, then you have already won because anyone who is striving for a high level of achievement and is on track to get there has already won the race. They have already played out the moment of victory in their minds well before it comes time to perform. You see this high frequency in musicians, dancers, athletes, and martial artists. They have rehearsed and performed, both physically and mentally, over and over again until the moves are second nature. What begins in their minds moves outward to become manifest in their bodies and in their lives.

When you live in the mental space of high frequency, you will perform accordingly. When the curtains draw, you will step out onto the stage, get into the flow, and your success will certainly unravel before you.

CHAPTER SIX
Physical Frequency

The certainty of your success begins in your spirit, moves into your mind, and then continues outward until it is manifest in your physical reality. However, these manifestations flow both ways. Your physical reality, or your physical frequency, also influences the frequency of your mindset and your spirit—as it does all of your frequencies. You can see this pattern by looking at your own life. Think of a time when you felt phenomenal, like you could do anything. You were in the zone. You were fully in that space where everything you put your mind to was easily accomplished. Your senses were so sharp that any obstacle or task to be overcome seemed to come at you in slow motion—you were able to move through it and beyond with almost no effort at all.

Now think of a time when you were sick and exhausted. The simple act of getting out of bed seemed insurmountable, and you viewed the hours ahead with dread. The basic tasks of the day were enough to overwhelm you and cause you to feel frustrated or depressed. You inevitably had to dial down and conserve your energy for the basic functions of survival. Eat. Sleep. Rest.

Your body is like the home in which you live, sleep, and raise your family. A house that is not taken care of will betray you and fall in on itself because that frequency will bring what it brings. If you keep it nasty, it is going to bring in some other things that you didn't invite to live with you. They are going to live there with you, and they are going to disrupt you and share in everything that you share in, whether it be a rodent or insect. Your physical frequency affects the way that you think and go out into the world and how you send others out into the world, whether it be your children, employees, or anyone else you are responsible for. It is deeply tied in to your other frequencies—your spiritual life, your mindset, your relationships, how you show up in the world, and how you're compensated for showing up.

But if you look at the human body, it always chooses life. Its job is simple—to live, to thrive, to grow, to experience, to learn, and to reach for the sun. *Your* job is to learn how to give your body what it needs in order to do that.

High Physical Frequency = Health

The life force of your body is equivalent to its health. The person at a high frequency is healthier than a person who is at a low frequency. I mean this quite literally. You can actually measure the frequency in the human body. You have impulses of energy and electricity flowing through your body that keep you alive and are part of living. For instance, an EKG measures the electrical output of your heart. Everything in your body is always moving. Even when a person leaves this earth and makes his or her final transition, the body still emits a frequency as it decays and returns to dust. Energy always moves, and we are energetic beings.

In 1992, Bruce Tainio, renowned biologist and founder of Tainio Technology, invented the first frequency monitor in the world. He was able to measure the frequencies of the energy running through the brain, lungs, liver, pancreas, each of the body's glands, and more. Every cell in every part of your body is emitting a frequency right now, as do all living things. Tainio compared and contrasted his readings between healthy and unhealthy individuals. His research determined that during the day, a normal human body's frequency is between sixty-two and sixty-eight megahertz.

He found that when that frequency drops, the body's immune system is compromised. However, when your body's frequency stays over that sixty-two-megahertz mark, you aren't likely to get sick as often because your immune system is strong. Health and disease have different frequencies. When you take medications or administer different treatments, you are administering a frequency to get something else to move or respond in order to remove your symptoms.

People often live their physical lives at an unsteady, unpredictable frequency because they don't know how to tap in to a higher, healthier frequency and stay there. They are either there or they're not. When they aren't, they don't know why. When they are, they still don't know why. Their paths just happen to cross into a higher frequency by chance, and they don't have the resources to live there. They don't have the information to self-correct and to understand they have to link in with the frequencies that we are talking about in this book. All of these frequencies all work in harmony together, and they all have to be aligned with each other.

How to Raise Your Physical Frequency

There are several ways you can move your body into a higher physical frequency. In the next chapter, we will fully explore the principles on which your body operates so that you can master them for the long run. But first, I will give you a brief list of practices that will immediately change your state and move you into a higher frequency at any given moment.

Earthing

We live in a world full of frequencies, energy, and vibrations, and we are a part of that whole system. Our bodies come from the earth and live in harmony with it, not separate from it. As you walk barefoot across the surface of this planet, its energy feeds yours. More specifically, its *correcting* yours. When you come into direct contact with the earth, you pick up a negative charge through its free electrons, which neutralizes the positive charges of the unhealthy free radicals you pick up throughout your day. Those positive charges come from all around you in a variety of ways. For instance, they come from sitting in front of your computer screen, eating microwaved foods, and being exposed to pollutions and pesticides—just to name a few. These free radicals accelerate the breakdown of your body, increase your stress, and are contributors to disease. Luckily, the world you live in comes with quick and natural antidotes for these free radicals.

When I first learned about earthing, it made perfect sense to me. I thought about how the earth feeds the soil and the seed, creating and sustaining life. Think of all the insects, worms, and other living things that burrow and live below the soil. All of these things live below the surface, and when they break through or walk out into the light of day, they are drawing energy from the sun. We, too, can and should tap in to these sources of power and energy.

The next time you step outside in the summertime and walk around in the grass with naked feet while the sun is out there shining, close your eyes and feel your body relax as you draw this healing energy in. You can compare this to the homes and devices that run on solar power. The panels drink in the energy that is being put out there by the sun, and then they can tap in to that energy and put it to use as their own. Your body is no different. There is a healing energy running through this entire planet all the way down to the core. Energy cannot be created or destroyed, but it can certainly be shared. As a human being, you can tap in to that force and redirect it through your life to raise your frequency.

Eat Living Foods

When you eat living foods, you are carrying this same healing energy into your body by way of your mouth. By definition, living foods have *life* in them. They have a higher frequency and energy vibration than dead, processed, and overly-cooked foods. Everything you take in to your body has a ripple effect. Life breeds life. Death breeds death.

Remember, we are all part of everything. The trees around us produce oxygen, and we rely on that oxygen to live. The earth produces our food—our fruits, vegetables, and seeds. Without that, we don't have access to the nourishment we need. Even if you choose to consume meat, these are animals that survived by living off the earth. When you get your nutrients from animals, you are getting them secondhand. You will get a higher quality of nutrients and energy by eating primary sources of energy, which are living plants.

Laughter

You can immediately step into a higher frequency through laughter. Laughter releases endorphins and is a great way to reboot or recharge. When I am speaking to large groups, I do an exercise in which I have everyone laugh hysterically for ten seconds. It is so amazing to witness the way it changes the charge in the whole room. At the end of the talk, some of the most successful people in the room say, "I can't believe that I am this accomplished CEO or doctor and you had me laughing like that! I came here to get some information, but the way you gave it to us was an experience I will never forget." I appreciate that because the experience is by design. I aim to get their body charged up physically in order to reboot and recalibrate their entire state.

The physical practice of laughter creates a powerful chain of reactions in your body. Among other things, laughter decreases pain, helps digestion, and boosts your immune system. This is true even in the absence of humor. For instance, if you're sitting at your desk and feeling down, or if you are feeling the stress of the day crushing in on you, you can immediately change your state by laughing. Laugh hard and long. Even if you don't find the practice particularly funny and you're just going through the motions because Mr. Dentley said you should, the laughter will still move you into a space of higher physical frequency.

Mantras and Declarations

It has been written that, "Thou shall decree a thing and that it shall be established unto you, and it will accomplish that to where it has been sent." When you speak a declaration, it is a statement of your intentions in the world. This can be one powerful sentence, or several. It is you speaking your truth, and it will resonate throughout your being, pulling you forward into a higher state.

When you speak a mantra, it is the repetition of a word or phrase, over and over again. Its intonation becomes music.

You want to have mantras and declarations for everything because they tap in to the frequency of your body, mind, and spirit. As you speak the words, you are engaging your body in several ways. The tone of your voice, the hum of the words, the breath moving through your body, the images flashing through your mind, your heart rate as you experience the certainty of your intentions—all of these increase your physical frequency. When you speak from your heart and from the fabric of your being, you activate a higher level of frequency.

Here is an example of a declaration:

Today I make a declaration that my body is my temple and my castle. It is my home, and I will live in it for the rest of my life that I have consciousness. So, I will keep it clean because I know a clean house is a better energy force. I declare in this day that I will move in alignment with my Higher Power, and with the frequency that resides in me and all around me. I will be in tune with the earth. I will now on this day recognize and take a moment to take a deep breath of fresh air and admire the sun. The sun will shine around me today as I tap in to the energy resource that the sun brings and which powers even the homes and the factories that exist in our world today. I will admire and appreciate the grass, the trees, the animals, and all things that live.

I understand that I can tap in to an area of higher performance, and this day I will strive to do so. If I am able to take the stairs instead of the elevator, I will take the stairs. If the climb is too steep, I will take some stairs and ride the rest of the way. If I can't do a lot, then I will do a little. I will no longer take the easy way out because the world depends upon me. I need my body to perform for me because it affects my mental state and all other areas of frequency in my life. It shows up in my relationships and my financial world. Abundance is coming to me this day because I am in alignment with my body and the highest frequency accessible to me, and which has always been accessible to me. The power to life itself is here every single day, so this day I make a declaration that I am in alignment, and I will live my dreams and accomplish my goals. I will create new goals and dreams that will take me even farther, and there will be no limits to my living.

Meditation

Meditation is a powerful tool you can use to bring your body, heart, and spirit into tune with each other on a higher frequency. It creates a stillness in your life that allows you to walk between the gaps of what you perceive and tap in to the power to create. This stillness is so important because it allows you to slow down and view your own existence in motion. When you are able to witness the unfolding moments of that motion, you can direct that motion with your power of thought and intention.

When it comes to governing your physical frequency, it really starts with the way you choose to think about it. Your thoughts govern the actions you take and the reality that is manifest. That's why one person can have the ability to endure more pain than another person, and why you can either talk and think yourself into being sick or into being at peak performance.

When I was studying martial arts, we had moments of meditation where we had to learn to breathe. We would begin by coming solidly into the present moment where we rest as a physical being. Then we would move into tension exercises by drawing tension into our arms to build muscle, and then push out the breath. Then we would breathe back in with a fluid, soft, beautiful inhale of that essence of life and energy. We would do these exercises to the point that I believed I could hear an ant walking around on the group. I would open my eyes and sure enough, there would be an ant there.

Your breath is your life force, and it weaves through every one of your frequencies. As you meditate, you are able to focus on that force and draw it in with intention, letting the energy of the universe infuse you with light and healing, and then exhale, allowing that breath to carry out the blocks in your frequency.

Meditating does not always mean you will be sitting on the side of a hill in the Lotus position. You may not be sitting at all. Ultimately, it is a practice of stillness, presence, and release. Eventually, you will be able to go to that space and to that frequency at will, whether it be in the middle of an argument, while trying to make difficult decisions, or at the cusp of giving up in the gym. I had a personal trainer who told me that while I was training and my body began to hurt, I should simply say, "Thank you, pain. I am glad you are here. Thanks for letting me know I am alive. I know it hurts, and I know you are trying to get me to stop, but I am going to take it from here." That is a perfect example of meditation on the go.

Music

Studies show that listening to music lights up the whole brain, the driver of your body. Music is a powerful tool that affects your frequency in an instant, as it affects the way you feel and sends numerical patterns throughout your body. Think of a particular song that completely transports you to a specific time and place. You can see what you saw the first time you heard it. You can smell what you smelled. You are the same age, wearing the same thing, doing the same things, and feeling the same things. Perhaps it was your first kiss or a time when you lost someone close to you. It could plunge you into despair, or it could excite you. You have had many experiences in your life that demonstrate the power of music.

You should be very intentional about the music that you invite into your space. Seek out the music that reflects the state you are seeking. You can easily identify the frequencies of music because you can feel them. If you are stressed, seek out calming, classical music. If you need motivation to move, find music that will pump you up and pull you off of the couch.

You can use each of these tools and practices to make an immediate shift in your physical state and frequency. However, for a more long-term, stable frequency to be maintained, you will need to do some deep recalibrations. I will now share with you the five truths that are governing your physical frequency at all times. These are relatively unknown facts that will totally redirect your understanding of health. Understanding and applying these truths will position you to take your body to the highest frequency possible.

CHAPTER SEVEN
The 5 Truths of Physical Frequency

Now I am going to share with you the five truths that direct your physical frequency. These facts of health will be presented in an easy-to-understand format so you can put them into practice right away. However, I have to warn you that mastering these truths requires a paradigm shift on your part. In order to prepare for that shift, you must keep an open mind as you move forward. If you can do that, you will be able to digest this new information, which will give you a transforming understanding of health. Internalizing these truths will reveal to you a whole new side of health that will impact the way you live, promote your optimum health, and give you a new sense of clarity and focus.

The 5 Truths of Physical Frequency are:
1. Your body is designed for addiction.
2. Your body is trained for success.
3. The intake of food is a master trainer for human choice and selection. It can teach you to transform from choices made towards survival to making life choices or choices that build.
4. Exercise should not be about weight loss as much as it should be about creating memory in the body.

5. Your health is more about what you can accomplish in your life and your relationships than it is about diet and exercise.

As you internalize these five truths, you will be able to manipulate them to your benefit and to increase your frequency.

1. Your body is designed for addiction.

Health is what your body remembers it to be. That's it. Most of what you do in life is done in support of your health or the state of your health, whether it's good or bad, optimum or non-optimum. You follow what your body remembers itself to be. So, where does this memory come from? Repetition and the multiplication and transfer of information on the most fundamental levels. Fundamentally, it comes from addiction.

Most people and healthcare professionals believe that addiction is a function of the brain. To some degree it is, but addiction is actually primarily housed in, and a direct function of, the body—not the brain. Medically, a good part of your body is developed well before your brain during fetal development. When it comes to your feelings, your hormones and neurotransmitters, which are located both in your brain and body, are calling the shots. However, the place where you feel pain, joy, fear, love, rejection, ecstasy, and most other emotions are felt primarily in the body. In addition, any persistence of negative emotions destroys the body first and not the brain. Therefore, the hold of any addiction is experienced in the body and not the brain. Why is this important? What does this have to do with your overall health? Remember that your body is created as an instrument for success. Its development began several billion years ago[1] and has intentionally evolved into its present state in

---

[1] **The Biblical Account**

Here, I must be sensitive to those who come from a strong religious background that promotes the idea that the earth and all that was created

which it is designed to create a multiplicity of things. Your body knows how to win.

Let me explain.

2. Your body is trained for success.

Your body is literally designed for your success. The human system—physiologically, emotionally, and mentally—is designed to create and manifest your spiritual desires. When you set your intention, whatever it is, a special set of genes in your body is then geared to accomplish what you want. When you state a desire, your physical body maps a frequency to that exact desire or space. Your hippocampus, which is a part of your brain, has cells in it called place cells, which are designed to take in information. As the place cell takes in the information of the route you need to move along, it sets it to become memory via your hormone glutamate. This information becomes stored so that it can communicate and teach your other cells to comply with what's wanted.

To do this, your body must remember to properly transport electrons. Otherwise your health will fail. You will recall from high school science classes that it is primarily the number of protons and electrons that give elements their definition. Just as electrons give definition to all the elements such as gold, sulfur, hydrogen, oxygen, magnesium, and the like; electrons also give definition to the what

---

happened within a literal succession of seven periods of twenty-four hours, and that the earth is 6,000 to 10,000 years old. I'm not stating the ideas in this chapter in the spirit of debate or to dispute the Biblical account. Rather, it is my intention to expand your consciousness and introduce another level of awareness to you. Personally, I believe the Biblical account, but feel strongly that the account recorded in Genesis should be read in its correct context. Time as we define it exists as a result of the sun, moon, and stars. These didn't exist until the fourth day, age, or eon. Therefore, there's no way a 24-hour day existed, so all the accounts before then can't be measured in traditional time. I believe the Genesis story actually mirrors evolution.

you want in life and the resulting state of your body. The best use of electrons is to make sure that they have something to do. This is the basis of all life function. Electrons roaming free in your body are the basis to mostly all diseases, body breakdowns, low-energy states, and illnesses. To ensure your body is running on all cylinders, your body must remember how to properly manage these electrons.

So, memory is the key to all of life. Your body has spent nearly five billion years learning exactly what to do with itself, and addiction is simply tying yourself into what you believe is necessary for you to stay alive (its first priority), and to have the best experiences possible (its second priority). In this way, addiction is a cycle of your body. First, it puts you in an ideal state of possessing a desire, and then your body pursues that desire. It's been doing this from the earliest cell formations billions of years ago, all the way to your present body. Your body specifically knows how to be successful, and it uses addiction as a point of getting there.

Inherently, there's nothing wrong with addiction. Your body is designed to be addicted to the creative points that come out of your mind. In general, your body's cells like to be told what to do. Your cells have what you call receptors and these receptors are attached to strands of proteins that pierce every cell. Chemicals attach themselves to these receptors, which then send messages through the cell. Cells talk to each other and have a language all their own. Cells learn from other cells, and then cells learn from outside stimuli. Before approximately 10,000 years ago, cells got their instruction from environmental factors: weather conditions, the state of the environment, predators, the time of day, the time of year, photosynthesis, etc. It was after that time that man began to receive instructions to cells via a new option—an idea.

A man's dream, desire, or destiny sent chemicals shooting through the body, attaching itself to cell receptors proclaiming, "We're going to be this or that." The cells were already trained to be in agreement with the chemicals as man began to dream of futures, and the body was smart enough to stage a plan of support for outward accomplishment.

Anything that is to be accomplished must be accomplished on the inside first (this is where your spirit and your mindset tie in). Anything that is desired, the body's cells, via chemical messages, will say yes to this new atmospheric environment of mental creations that then drive the body to the accomplishment of that desire. In essence, in order to accomplish anything, you must feel like accomplishing it. Once you affectively feel the accomplishment, the memory of what you want is built into your body via the energy production of the electron transport chains, and every morning you drive yourself to your destiny. Addiction.

From Addiction to Addiction

However, we do not generally use the mechanisms of addiction to accomplish our intentional goals. Most people do not even know addiction can be used in this way. Let me explain.

Traditional diet and exercise are opportunities to create habits of success, growth, and transformation in the body. These small increments of success entrain the body for successes outside of the body. Food intake and the hormones excreted during exercise send healthy doses of hormones to attach to your cell receptors.

Every time you exchange with another human, you secrete hormones and neurotransmitters that attach to your cell receptors. Remember, your body is looking to complete successful patterns, so you must measure and monitor your exchanges with each other and measure your accomplishments. These have a much more acute and direct impact on your health than diet and exercise.

When you do not practice these important factors, your body still needs to feel complete. Most ingest illicit drugs or pharmaceuticals, which also attach to cell receptors. What happens here is that the success is not processed through the body before the hormones and neurotransmitters attach to receptors in the brain. This gives a euphoric experience, but without actual processes that lead to the same psychological space. The brain gets it, but the body doesn't. So, the body in turn craves the experience again. That's why addiction is a function of the body and not the brain. Once a cycle of need is created in the body, the brain has no choice but to follow.

Cells that expect serotonin ingested through food, which is designed to support your success genes, will get alcohol, opiates, nicotine, and other narcotics to continue a pattern of memory built in to the body. The strongest addictive substance is sugar, which is seven times more addictive than cocaine and heroin. Food is addictive because it is the easiest process to complete and get an immediate sense of accomplishment. You've probably seen or experienced cases of what is called stress eating, where you eat just because you want to feel different. As human beings, most of the things we do, we do because we want to feel different. We want to escape a feeling or grab on to a feeling—a feeling that has a memory—that gives us something that makes us not have to deal with the realities of what is really going on in our lives. When people are dying in the body, they eat to mask the truth of this. The energy timing for all of these diminished cycles are short and must be experienced again and again to feel accomplished. The worst danger to your health is to feel accomplished without actually being accomplished.

The definition of illness or pain is the difference between where you are and where you are designed to be. If you are living a life void of accomplishment, then you are not living out your purpose as a human, and your body will then begin to break down. If there is no dream, the body is left to accept the ingestion of outside stimuli to make it feel successful. This is when life gets really sad.

Results and accomplishment are a necessary function of your health. You are either growing and transforming into greater existences, or you are dying. The inception of either path begins with the nature of your food intake.

3. The intake of food is a master trainer for human choice and selection.

I want to call all food nutritional intake. All of your food habits are centered in the area of your brain called the Food Entraining Oscillator (FEO), and then you have your twenty-four-hour night/day, sleep/awake behaviors that are controlled in the Super-chiasmatic Nucleus (SCN) of the brain. Your food selections and the time you eat become entrained in your brain and are the original source of your personal selection processes. Both in evolution and within early child development, food is the very first opportunity for you to exercise your power of choice. It is the progenitor of all your other selection processes and how you make choices. When it comes to food selection and the time that you eat, food selection and timing actually teaches you how to make choices and then set those same choices or selections into extended behavioral practices. Science calls this Long-Term Potentiation (LTP).

Think about it: Throughout early biological processes up until now, food intake has been your chief and primary point of survival. Food has always been about survival for all living species. You have to eat to live. Historically, a major part of all life was about hunting and gathering for nutritional sustenance. Eat or die. It was the need for sustenance and nutrition that pushed the development of our species. Even though you are no longer dependent on hunting and gathering, your need for food is still a steering mechanism for your body and your life.

What you eat is, of course, important. The food you choose is the fuel you're running on. However, the act of selection and eating itself, regardless of the "what," produces ripple effects in your body and throughout your life. The nature and the timing of your food choices create rhythms and cycles in your body, which touch every other function of your body and your life. When you eat food at certain times during the day, your body begins to take measure of your mealtimes and the food entrained oscillators (FEO) begin to create timing systems to help your body to anticipate mealtimes each day. This creates what we will call "body clocks." Your brain and body contain clocks called circadian rhythms. These are in all of your cells and tissues. These rhythms, although in different parts of your body and brain, will begin to line up if they are trained to do so. They come from a special set of genes that make sure that your body produces these clocks, which help your body to complete things. These genes have been termed by a close friend of mine as "Success Genes." They are part of the blueprint your body carries on exactly how to be successful.

The circadian rhythms time out the starting and completion of many processes within your body, including:

- Sleep and awake cycles
- Dietary cycles
- Menstrual cycles
- Conception and birthing
- Heart rate
- Respiration rate

As your body successfully goes through each of these processes and cycles, it trains your body for success. Your body is used to producing and being successful. The circadian rhythms are a function of memory, and remember that health is simply what your body remembers to be. Food selection and timing is the beginning of this training. Of all the processes in your body affected by cycles and rhythm, what sets the food, nutritional, or dietary cycles apart is that they are the only ones that involve human choice or selection. Those choices, in turn, create rhythms. The power you have to create these rhythms is a gift and should be exercised with care and intention. It is vital that you begin to understand this.

Nutritional habits should not be about weight loss or just physical health. Your first gift is to train your body for success through good habits, therefore creating circadian clocks and rhythms that support success not just in your body, but in every single other area of your life. Here, you are not training the body to be healthy—you are teaching your body to be successful. Herein lies the gift: when your body learns success and the circadian rhythms line up to that success, then those same rhythms and processes continue outside of your body and apply to your entire physical reality. Remember that your dream is a spiritual seed that grows into outward success. These rhythms are the vehicle of that success.

Let me put it another way. When you choose or select a desire, and then after a certain amount of time find yourself not accomplishing that desire, it is because your body doesn't know how. It has no memory of how to accomplish that goal and is therefore unable to create the necessary energy for its accomplishment. Think of a time when you have woken up and did not feel like doing the very things you said you were going to do the night before, or when you started your day with full anticipation of completing your to-do list, but then you end the day having accomplished nothing on your list. You may attribute these realities to procrastination, but in reality, there is no such thing as procrastination. There is only your body remembering how to move forward or not remembering how to move forward. You are not necessarily putting things off as much as you just have no memory of how to accomplish them.

This principle bleeds over into your financial health, as well. If you get up in the morning and you want to make fifteen thousand dollars, but you only make one hundred fifty dollars, it is not that you can't make the fifteen grand; it is that your body doesn't know how to make it. Your body only knows how to make a hundred fifty dollars, so that's what it's going to create. Your body carries all of that information, all of that memory, at a cellular level. Health is about what you train your body to accomplish. This is why losing weight can never be an accomplishment, as it can only be a result of you training your body to do something in terms of better performance.

You can build this system of accomplishment and memory—of winning—through your simplest selection processes. You can train your body through diet on how to be successful, and your body then takes those entrained processes and applies it to anything else you choose or want to accomplish. For example, when it comes to money, some people make eight dollars an hour, and some people make upwards of thirty thousand dollars an hour, which makes them a decent millionaire. Some people, like Oprah, make upwards of three hundred thousand dollars an hour, every day, all day. The difference between the person making eight dollars and the person making hundreds of thousands is that one has a better grip on timing and rhythms than the other. One understands cycles and frequencies and the production within those cycles better than the other.

Choose Living Foods

The circadian rhythms know how to time out the success and accomplishment of what you want. This begins by selecting optimal foods that contribute to the success of your body. The foods you eat affect your body's rhythm and frequency. You can eat foods that make you feel sluggish and slow you down, make you depressed, or have an impact on the quality of your sleep. Or you can eat high-frequency foods that will move your entire body into a higher frequency. When you are in alignment with the frequency of your body and its energy and life force, you understand that you want to eat live food as much as possible because they have a high energy, and therefore feed your high energy. As you use them as the major source of fuel, you are able to consistently operate and perform on a very high level.

When you talk about the body's frequency, it is about moving forward with intention. You are moving towards a specific lifestyle on purpose and by choice. It won't happen overnight, but a lifestyle that promotes putting more life into your life will bring you more into harmony in all areas of your life. I lost over 100 pounds, and now I look good and my clothes fit well. I had to throw or give away all of my clothes. I eat, think, live and am different. I show up different because my physical frequency touches every other frequency in my life.

Stop disappointing or miss-appointing your body. It is your first opportunity to learn how to win. People pay thousands of dollars to go to motivational seminars and performance training events. Once the event is over, after a few days, they are back into the same old patterns. Decide now to break your patterns and set your physical frequency on a new trajectory. Detoxing the body can help you raise your frequency and get rid of the blockages that old patterns and junk foods have created in your body. You are going to live in that body of yours for the rest of your life. You might as well clean it up from time to time and take good care of it.

Your food entrained oscillators are one of the keys to winning, and your metabolism is a timing system that's mirrored in all areas of your life. It is vital that you treat these systems with respect and use them with intention and care. Exercise works the same way.

4. Exercise is not for weight loss, but for creating memory in the body.

You should not exercise to lose weight. Weight loss should be seen as nothing more than a natural byproduct of moving into higher frequencies. So, if exercise isn't about weight loss, what it is about? It is about performance. It is about learning to perform at a higher level—to be pushed and driven outside of the mental restraints and constraints that we have given ourselves. You exercise to train your body to be successful and create cycles of success.

I will give you an example. When I started training with a personal trainer, I was losing weight rapidly, and I really wanted to keep that going. One day, we are riding the bikes together, and he tells me that he is going to get me to the point where I am going to do one thousand crunches in one day. I am feeling good while I am pedaling away on the bike. I don't have any pain, and I am feeling accomplished by everything I have already done. This allows me to be able to suspend my disbelief and look ahead at the possibility of doing one thousand crunches and smile. I say, "Yes, I can see that."

Well, I have no idea that he means he is going to get me to that point *this day*. This is my first day back in the gym in over a year and a half. But I do it. Then, once my body has a memory of that, I know it can be done. The next day, I do two thousand crunches. Under his direction, I repeat these kinds of feats over and over. I go from swimming no laps in the pool, to swimming five laps in one day. I am in a continuous cycle of pushing my muscles to do things that they normally wouldn't be able to do, and which I didn't previously believe was even possible. This series of wins don't just reform my body—they reform my life.

Because I am feeling good about myself and what I have accomplished, I naturally begin to rise up and tap in to a frequency of high performance in different areas of my life. My body is in agreement with my mind and my financial goals and my spiritual goals. I become even more loving and more open and more expressive because all of our frequencies are intertwined. When you raise one, the others follow.

When you start getting into alignment with the frequency of conscious health, you are able to press forward in a different way and manner than you did before, and then this new way becomes familiar to your body. For example, let's say you set a goal to do ten thousand steps a day for fifteen days. By the fifth day, it's taking you an hour and fifteen minutes. Each day, you're moving more briskly and by day ten, you are hitting your mark within an hour. By day fifteen, you are walking at high speed completing your desired cycle in forty-five minutes, or maybe you are even jogging and hitting all ten thousand steps within twenty minutes. The idea here in completing your desired cycles, you are challenging yourself to complete the cycle faster and faster. Once you have mastered any personal cycle, the challenge is about your body agreeing with you. When your body is in agreement with your desire, your body is going to give you the tools to complete the cycle faster. It knows how to do that. You are never building muscle. Your body is giving the muscles what it needs to do things faster the next time. That's the secret of the body, and that's the secret of raising your frequency in all things.

That's what health is about. If you learn how to perform, then your body is going to give you the body to perform. You don't even have to ask. If I walk forty minutes today, when I wake up tomorrow, my body is going to say, "I can do that same distance in thirty minutes today," and the muscles, the heart rate, and the adrenaline will be there to do it. However, if you allow yourself to get distracted and you don't take advantage of the resources and the opportunity that your body has given you, you will atrophy back into a low energy state. You will cause disease because you just disobeyed your potential.

Once your body and muscles have a memory of being at a higher frequency, you will naturally be able to do things faster and easier. Exercise teaches your body how to perform, which in turn teaches *you* to perform. It is easy to see this cause and effect physically. When you exercise, your body releases endorphins, which helps create a healthy addiction. When you feel that way, you want to keep that feeling. You will look for other ways to retain that state. You will want to eat different. You decide you don't want the hamburger after all because you don't want to lose the ground you have gained. When you're choosing better nutritional intake, all of your biological processes work better. You are able to starve off depression, headaches and chronic fatigue. This creates more space for your spirit and your mind to flourish. The energy that was once being invested into suffering is now invested into creation and developing your ideas. All these things work together, and they work together for your good.

The reverse is also true. If you don't push your body to perform at a high frequency, you sink into a low physical frequency and your body starts to break down. It will begin to call out to you in the form of disease and fatigue. Then you pull your energy inward. You rob your relationships and the manifestations of your success of the life force they need to successfully perpetuate and instead invest that life force into your own survival. Your life will begin to crumble. It is like the nerves that web through your body. Nerves send out electrical pulses through your body, but imagine if one is a little clogged or disrupted. Imagine if the current or frequency of electricity is disrupted. You are still getting electricity through it, but you are not getting the maximum input and output that you were designed to have. It is the same way with your body. It creates a domino effect across all of your frequencies.

This is why being sick is never a good reason to stay on the couch. The opposite is true. When you see your immune system folding, that should be your primary indicator that it's time to change your state—not feed the state you're in. You can tell your future if you are willing to write it. Tap in to that frequency of imagination until you can believe, without a doubt, that your body can achieve amazing things, and it will.

Regardless of where you are starting out today, you are able to begin the act of pressing forward. It doesn't matter if you smoke, if you have disease, or if you are completely out of shape. I have seen all different kinds of people press forward, regardless of their present circumstances. You can press forward into a new space of higher physical frequency. This very important, and every individual has to find his or her own journey. You don't have to be in perfect shape, but you had better know how to operate. You have to start going in that direction.

However, nutrition or dietary concerns play only a small role in health. Food intake and exercise is the elementary entrainment system because it is only a model and an evolutionary precursor to the most vital entrainment system to your health and wealth, which is the nutritional intake of your relationships.

CHAPTER EIGHT
The Fifth Truth: Relationships

Your relationships and their resulting exchanges have a bigger impact on your body's circadian rhythms, RNA, DNA, hormones, and neurotransmitters than you can ever imagine, which is the basis of the fifth truth governing your physical frequency:

5. Your health is more about what you can accomplish in your life and your relationships than it is about diet and exercise.

In the Harvard Study of Adult Development, researchers tracked the lives of seven hundred and twenty-four men for over seventy-five years. They found that the single most important factor to someone's longevity was not their cholesterol or diet, but the quality of their relationships. It is our dietary selection of people that makes the biggest contribution to our overall frequency of health.

You must become acutely aware of this fact and treat these rhythmic energies as a dietary existence. Then you have to select what is ingested into your energy space, which will eventually become a habit within your own body. For example, when people procrastinate or can't make the necessary moves towards accomplishment, I can readily point out four or five people that they are in a relationship with that carry the habit of not doing anything. This then becomes the energy investment they are receiving into themselves. They have actually become what their friends are.

Circadian rhythms synchronize. They are designed just for that—choices. If the process of not making a decision keeps going over time, your insulin production in your pancreas will be interrupted over time, your insulin production in your pancreas will be interrupted. When more time passes, your blood will turn into syrup and your cells cannot process sugar into energy. Diabetes did not start in the pancreas. It started within the low energy relationships where production was not a priority. So it is with other health issues.

I can assure you that by the time cancer, heart disease, renal kidney issues, diabetes, hypertension, or any of these diseases hit your body, the pattern or the frequency of that illness has already been going on outside of your body for a while. The frequency of your body broadcast the frequency of the disease, literally calling for it to come. There is an expanded configuration of activities and existences outside of your body that determines your state of health well before it becomes evident through an illness in your body. As a matter of fact, we use medicine to treat the illness without realizing that illness is just a behavior that eventually mirrors itself in the body at some point.

Here is the point of health: What you want in life is pivotal to your personal health. At one point in human history, an individual's health was driven by the environment. Now your health is driven by your choices, both as it concerns your desires and as it concerns the relationships surrounding your desires.

Health is also driven by your accomplishments in life. What you finish and achieve contributes to the function of your body by encoding the information of your cycles of completion directly into your DNA through cell messaging.

Yes, nutrition is a precursor training to your true health, but it is a small role compared to starting and finishing something you desire. That is the whole point of life, is it not? Your health needs results. As humans, we are a species that uses its hormones, neurotransmitters, and circadian structures to both grow the body to maturation, and then use those same biological structures to push development outside of the body. This development comes in the form of businesses, wealth, dreams, desires, material accumulation, relationships, etc. When your body needs to move to an additional stage of development, or to a different frequency, it secretes the necessary hormones and chemicals that will initiate that process. It does the exact same thing when you desire something. This is why you cannot be truly healthy without a dream. Dreams are a necessary trigger to your continual growth and transformation. Then those same hormones, neurotransmitters, and circadian rhythms transfer to pushing growth, transformation, and production outside of the body.

Transformation vs. Growth

All biological life extends from this notion of transformation. Transformation is the essence of all life. Most people use the term "growth," but if you look closer at biological life, what you are actually witnessing is transformation. A seed does not grow into a tree or a plant. A seed *transforms* through a series of stages to *become* a tree or a plant. As previously discussed, your desires are seeds of your spirit and go through a similar process of transformation, so when it comes to personal growth and transformation, you can draw an analogy from the patterns we see in all of biology.

It is important to understand this process as transforming stages versus growth stages. A tree is not growing as much as it is transforming from pre-determined stage to pre-determined stage—but only as it is given what it needs to facilitate that transformation. You are the only species that continues to transform beyond your biological processes. It's a guarantee that is built in your body-brain system. You are built for success. You are built for greatness. However, you must feed that potential with what nature demands in order for the right transformation to occur.

Understanding life and accomplishment from this standpoint sets you at an advantage when it comes to getting what you want. When you align the investments in your life to facilitate your transformation, transformation becomes a biological guarantee. Your body is designed to create the energy of what you want. In fact, when there is an energy shift in your direction and there becomes a difference between where you said you wanted to go or what you said you wanted to accomplish and what is actually happening, your cells become damaged because they are used to succeeding.

What has been designed to make your body what it is, is the same system used to accomplish your dreams, but you must, in the same way, build systems of communication that keep you on the frequency of your desire. The energy of exchanges within a relationship becomes highly directional because that is how frequency works. When people are having severe issues in life or in health, those issues are always mirrored in from a system of surrounding relationships. How others treat you and what they invest in you becomes you when you are in agreement with those treatments and investments. Therefore, you must take care in calibrating your relationships based on your pre-determined purpose, desires, and destiny in order to create the most optimum model for your transformation.

My good friend Les Brown, the number one motivational speaker in the world, always says when it comes to accomplishment, "You gotta be hungry!" In a great sense, he is absolutely right. One thing your body will not let you do is go without food. Your body has a specific hormone called ghrelin that lets you know that it is time to eat. It can only be satisfied by eating. Again, all of this is about time and production. This same process is transferred over to your desire. You have to be hungry for what you want, and that hungry will only go away when you get it. That satisfaction leaves your body in an optimum state. So you see, your optimum health is as closely tied to what's going on outside the body as it is to what's going on inside the body. The ability to dream, imagine, and set destinies or benchmarks contribute directly to your health, and then your daily actions that line up to your vision contributes to your health.

A desire is easy to set and will cause you to excrete hormones that will make you excited about what can be, but that potential can be killed by people who can't contribute or invest towards what you want. Your dream dies at the next person. This leads to diminished processes in the body that will eventually become a disease. Have you ever stepped away from a conversation with a person and felt stressed or fatigued for some reason? You never really know the frequencies and resulting rhythmic patterns you are picking up from others.

Menstrual cycles are a prime example of how circadian rhythms work and how this applies to your relationships and overall health. An egg is delivered every month to the uterus for fertilization. Within the few days of the eggs presence, if it is not fertilized, the egg spoils and blood will flow to wash out the spoiled egg. Likewise, when you have connected with another human, there always sits a potential between you and the other person. You must identify that potential and then come to an agreement to produce that potential. This is the same concept of fertilization. When the potential is not actuated, you are dealing with a spoiled person who could not be fertilized within a given time. The resulting feeling is stress.

This stress is not just something affecting your mind. It is the result of several biological processes in your body trying to clue you in to the nature of the relationship you are in. The blood in your body gives you the message to wash that person out of your life by doing the following: In the course of your relationship, your blood cells begin to swell because the gradient shifts in the cells, keeping the necessary ions out of your cells and the necessary water in your cells. This is called inflammation. So, the resulting feeling is stress because your body turns off the clocks or circadian rhythms and institutes new patterns of non-production. Your body also has vomit centers along the spine that help convey the message. These are designed to expel what doesn't work, meaning you can literally experience nausea when dealing with a spoiled person, just like when you take in spoiled food.

Your body is designed to expel what doesn't work and to allow cells to die (apoptosis, for you scientists), then create new cells that are waiting for you to ingest something new and nutritional. Eggs, which are simply cells, when unproductive, spoil and are washed away to make room for new eggs. You have cells that die daily to make room for new cells, giving you a chance to make new and better decisions for them to memorize. When you hold on to what doesn't work, your body memorizes cycles of death versus cycles of production. It's just like eating bad food over and over again, not allowing for new processes to be introduced. In order to maintain the highest physical frequency possible, you must release the relationships in your life that are killing you.

Connections with other people are symbiotic relationships—you give and you receive. It is important to be as aware of what you are putting out as what others are putting in. As a very good friend of mine says, "Love is investing yourself into someone's greatness, and taking responsibility for those investing into yours." You are designed for greatness, and all that you desire is within your power to create. However, what you manifest will be largely guided by the relationship investments you receive. How you allow people to treat you, engage with you, and to see you become you. This is a matter of biology, and is true for all life and development.

Without photosynthesis, for example, plants cannot develop. Most things can't grow without water, whether it comes from the ground, condensation in the form of dew, or rain falling from the sky. All of life's transformations come from outside investment—more particularly, specific transformations require specific investments. The same is true for your personal transformation. Just as a plant cannot decide to use oil instead of water to reach its biological peak, you cannot decide to just use what is in front of you to achieve your desired outcome. Your desire rests at a specific frequency, and requires a specific frequency of thought and action in order for it to be achieved. Oil cannot be water. The wrong people in your life cannot be the right people. Incompatible investments will not be compatible with your desired outcome. You have to set your intention, and then feed that intention with what nature demands.

The Object of Your Desire

To do this, you must be fiercely intentional in setting your course based on a fixed point—your static purpose and destiny. Never chase a relationship and design your destiny around that, or you will never experience a stable frequency. Frequencies are messed up when you make another person the object of your desire. Other humans are not designed as objects of desire. This is where most go wrong and end up in spaces and places where they don't want to be. Instead, the object of your desire should always be an immovable point or condition. Then, you must choose your relationships based on their ability to propel you toward that set point.

When another person becomes your goal, you are dealing with a moving target, and your destiny becomes arbitrary. This is why it's imperative to design your relationships around your destiny, versus designing your destiny around your relationships. To look at it from a spiritual point of view, God created things before He created people, and then He told man to master the things, and then He paired humans together. He created the relationship second. The purpose of the relationship is to help with the mastery or dominion of things, and not the other way around. Likewise, you must first set your course for your desired frequency and outcome, then create relationships with those who will move you in that direction. People who are not aligned with your desire, direction, and destiny will become a severe distraction to all three. You will be either influenced off track or distracted away from the right track. When you allow your relationships to change the channel of your frequency, you will eventually find yourself in an undesired space.

When I speak of spaces, I am referring to a better space, a different space, an assigned space, a new space, or a higher space. It could be the space of a career, finances, or a relationship. You can move from the space of one school to another, or from one class to another. You can be in the space of a particular religion, and then for whatever reason, desire to move into the space of a new or a more meaningful religion. Moving from your bed in the morning to the bathroom is moving from one space to another. You and I are constantly and consistently moving into different spaces.

Here is the key: Life is better when you take the time to intentionally design your movements throughout your spaces. People often take their movements in life for granted and end up in undesired places and spaces, especially when it comes to relationships.

For example, think of an older FM radios. Each station carries its own frequency. On that radio is a dial which lets you move from station to station or space to space. You can change the channel. People fail in life because they set a destiny based on what's in front of them—the resources available only on the frequency they're already on—then they are never able to change the channel. Or they successfully change the channel but get distracted by old patterns or people on the lower frequencies they are used to. Their intentional movement is sabotaged as they are either influenced out of, or distracted from, the space of their destiny. The channel is changed, and they unintentionally end up in a different space—a space where failure exists. This happens in the absence of awareness.

To illustrate my point, I will use the example of an airliner. When the pilot adjusts his instruments for a desired flight, the plane is set via frequencies to arrive at a very specific destination. The pilot then must keep the instruments carefully calibrated to an exact latitude and longitude in order to arrive at the desired destination. If the plane is off by one degree, it will reach an entirely different destination, or it won't reach a destination at all but will crash and burn. Likewise, to get where you have determined you want to, you must be immovable in your course and refuse to give place to the wrong investments that will indefinitely nudge you off course. Never allow another human to become the object of your ultimate desire. Humans are designed to create *things*, not other humans. As you set a desire to create a thing—a business, a purpose, a mission, a destiny—you then have the responsibility to arrange the investments coming into your life so that they will fortify your existence. You must ensure that the relationships you enter into are in agreement with your highest purpose and destiny in order for the space you're entering into to be fortified. The frequencies of your relationships must be monitored and measured.

The 12 Points of Significance

I have a friend who developed a system to do just this. This guide is called the 12 Points of Significance. These twelve points are the investments that you need to be looking for and monitoring in your relationships. As you use these as a guide, you do not have to rely so heavily on your subjective feelings, but will have an actual system for collecting data to determine whether or not you are on a compatible trajectory with the results that you want in your life.

The 12 Points of Significance are listed below and also described in more detail in the following tables:

- To Be Viewed: The Investment of seeing and knowing a person
- To Be Comprehended: The Investment of understanding a person
- To Be Engaged: The Investment of active commitment
- To Be Praised: The Investment of vocal affirmation of the good
- To Be Believed: The Investment of trust
- To Be Prioritized: The Investment of making one special
- To Be Enriched: The Investment of provision
- To Be Advanced: The Investment of pushing one forward
- To Be Rewarded: The Investment of active recognition
- To Be Exalted: The Investment of oneself into another
- To Be Increased: The Investment of addition
- To Be Doubled: The Investment of multiplication

The Fifth Truth: Relationships

THE NEED	THE INVESTMENT	DESCRIPTION	QUESTIONS TO MEASURE THE INVESTMENT
TO BE VIEWED	THE INVESTMENT OF SEEING AND KNOWING A PERSON	• TO KNOW A PERSON, AS IN THEIR HABITS, FAVORITE THINGS, CONCERNS, ETC. • TO BE CONCERNED ABOUT AND HAVING SOMEONE'S BACK BASED ON WHAT YOU SEE IN THEM. • TO SEE, RECOGNIZE, AND CARE FOR ONE'S ISSUES. • TO HAVE SOMEONE TO SEE AND KNOW WHO THEY ARE.	CAN THIS PERSON SEE WHO I AM?
TO BE COMPREHENDED	THE INVESTMENT OF UNDERSTANDING A PERSON	• UNDERSTANDING ONE'S ISSUES. • WILLINGNESS TO TAKE IN RIGHT INFORMATION CONCERNING A PERSON. • AGREEMENT AND RIGHT ACTION TOWARD THAT UNDERSTANDING OF THE PERSON. • FULFILLING EVERYONE'S NEED TO BE UNDERSTOOD.	DOES THIS PERSON UNDERSTAND ME?
TO BE ENGAGED	THE INVESTMENT OF ACTIVE COMMITMENT	• PHYSICAL CONNECTION AND INVESTMENT. • PARTNERSHIP AND UNIFICATION. • TWO-WAY EXCHANGE OR COMMUNICATION BETWEEN PEOPLE. • FULFILLING EVERYONE'S NEED TO BE TOUCHED IN SOME WAY.	DOES THIS PERSON ENGAGE WITH WHAT I'M TRYING TO ACCOMPLISH?
TO BE PRAISED	THE INVESTMENT OF VOCAL AFFIRMATION OF THE GOOD	• RECOGNITION AND HEARING ABOUT GOOD ATTRIBUTES. • BEING COMPLIMENTARY TOWARD A PERSON. • APPROVALS OF IDEAS, THOUGHTS, VISIONS, ETC. • FULFILLING EVERYONE'S NEED TO HEAR SOMETHING GOOD ABOUT HIS OR HERSELF.	AM I GETTING PRAISE OR AFFIRMATION FROM THIS INDIVIDUAL?

The 5 Frequencies of High Performance

THE NEED	THE INVESTMENT	DESCRIPTION	QUESTIONS TO MEASURE THE INVESTMENT
TO BE BELIEVED	THE INVESTMENT OF TRUST	• A POSITION BASED ON CONCERNS VERBALIZED, OR CHARACTER EXUDED. • ACTION-ORIENTED BELIEF QUALIFIED BY ACTION-ORIENTED SUPPORT. • TAKING RESPONSIBILITY AND ACTING ON A PERSON'S BEHALF BASED ON BELIEVING IN THEM. • FULFILLING EVERYONE'S NEED TO BE TRUSTED AND BELIEVED IN.	DOES THIS PERSON BELIEVE ME? DOES THIS PERSON BELIEVE IN WHAT I'M DOING?
TO BE PRIORITIZED	THE INVESTMENT OF MAKING ONE SPECIAL	• PAYING ACUTE ATTENTION IN CERTAIN SITUATIONS AND AREAS. • PUTTING THINGS ASIDE IN RECOGNITION OF THE OTHER. • ALLOWING A PERSON FROM TIME TO TIME TO BE THE MOST IMPORTANT. • FULFILLING EVERYONE'S NEED TO FEEL NO. 1 SOMETIMES.	AM I BEING PRIORITIZED? DOES THIS PERSON PUT ME FIRST?
TO BE ENRICHED	THE INVESTMENT OF PROVISION	• BRINGING GIFTS OR SUPPLIES NOT ASSOCIATED WITH EARNING. • SHARING YOUR PERSONAL SUBSTANCE. • MAKING SURE A PERSON'S NEEDS ARE MET. • FULFILLING EVERYONE'S NEED TO RECEIVE.	IS THIS PERSON MEETING MY NEEDS?
TO BE ADVANCED	THE INVESTMENT OF PUSHING ONE FORWARD	• PROGRESSING ONE'S EFFORT BY MEANS OF TIME AND EFFORTS. • PROVIDING LEADERSHIP IN YOUR AREA OF EXPERTISE TO ADVANCE THE CAUSE OF ANOTHER. • GIVING AN EFFORT IN SETTING A SITUATION OR CIRCUMSTANCE RIGHT. • FULFILLING EVERYONE'S NEED TO BE MENTORED OR PUSHED FORWARD.	IS THIS PERSON PUSHING ME TO THE NEXT LEVEL?

The Fifth Truth: Relationships

THE NEED	THE INVESTMENT	DESCRIPTION	QUESTIONS TO MEASURE THE INVESTMENT
TO BE REWARDED	THE INVESTMENT OF ACTIVE RECOGNITION	• TO PROVIDE SUBSTANCE IN RECOGNITION OF WHAT SOMEONE HAS INVESTED IN YOU. • TO PROVIDE PHYSICAL SUBSTANCE IN APPRECIATION FOR EFFORTS MADE. • TO PROVIDE THANK YOU AND APPRECIATION OUTSIDE OF VERBAL AFFIRMATION. • FULFILLING EVERYONE'S NEED TO BE APPRECIATED IN A TANGIBLE WAY.	DOES THIS PERSON APPRECIATE ME?
TO BE EXALTED	THE INVESTMENT OF ONESELF INTO ANOTHER	• TIME SPENT IN ALL AREAS OF EMOTIONAL INVESTMENTS. • A SENSE OF PLACE BASED ON YOUR PRESENCE. • THE GIFT OF YOURSELF THAT LIFTS A PERSON TO ANOTHER LEVEL, GIVES STATUS OR EMPOWERS. • FULFILLING EVERYONE'S NEED TO FEEL ANOTHER'S PRESENCE THAT BUILDS THEIR OWN PRESENCE.	DOES THIS PERSON SPEND SUFFICIENT TIME WITH ME TO MAKES A DIFFERENCE IN MY PROGRESS?
TO BE INCREASED	THE INVESTMENT OF ADDITION	• TO EMPOWER, ENHANCE OR ENABLE IN ANY WAY. • TO SEE THEN ADD IN A POSITIVE WAY TIME, EFFORT, OR SUBSTANCE. • TO BE AN EXTENSION FOR SOMEONE WHERE SOMEONE COMES SHORT. • FULFILLING EVERYONE'S NEED TO BE COMPLETED BY THE INVESTMENT OF ANOTHER'S EFFORT AND PARTNERSHIP.	AM I EMPOWERED BY THIS PERSON?
TO BE DOUBLED	THE INVESTMENT OF MULTIPLICATION	• THE EXPERIENCE OF RESULTS. • RESULTS THAT LEAD TO MORE RESULTS. • RESULTS THAT GIVE A SENSE OF PLACE, HOME, COMPLETENESS. • FULFILLING EVERYONE'S NEED TO GROW BY THE INVESTMENT OF ANOTHER'S EFFORT OR PARTNERSHIP.	CAN I SEE SOMETHING IN THIS PERSON THAT I SEE IN MYSELF?

Each of these twelve points are energy entry points, and they all stem from your relationships. You need all of these investments to have a complete sense of being, even if they are coming from a variety of people. One person may not contribute all twelve, but you should have the entire twelve being invested into your environment in order to make the environment compatible with the high frequencies you're aiming for.

All of your associations, whether they be relatives, business relationships, personal, or intimate relationships must be measured and monitored based on the investments you are receiving from them. You have to take responsibility of the investments made towards you from these associations, and there must be an expectation of premium behavior towards you in order to preserve and advance your personal well-being and wealth.

How to Measure Your Investments

In order to determine whether you are receiving all of the investments you need, write down a list of people you know including family, friends, lovers, and business relationships. Which of the twelve points does each individual contribute toward you? Study the table above and turn these twelve points into questions like those shown. You can use those exact questions as a guide, or you can create your own. Asking these questions is how you will monitor each person's level of participation in your life. What is his or her energy contribution to you? Is that person moving you closer to where you want to be, or is his or her frequency rerouting you somewhere else entirely?

It is difficult to look at your relationships objectively, but it is imperative that you do so on some level. What extends outside of yourself is commercial in every sense of the word, as these twelve points are points of commerce. The contributions you receive from others are ongoing energy lines that affect your thoughts, your movements, and your accomplishments. Furthermore, they feed into your sense of value. Remember, you must set your value and be confident in the value you set, which gives other people the opportunity to come into agreement with that value, or to keep moving. These energy entry points become the fuel for your transformation and must be well managed, as well as not taken for granted, for the investments you receive will determine the environment in which you are transforming, which defines what you will become in all things.

CHAPTER NINE
The Frequency
of Relationships

Once you have calibrated yourself on a high spiritual frequency, you are ready to show up and play as your best self in all of your relationships. Your mindset is also critical to this; in order to transform your relationships and bring them to a higher frequency, you have to recognize the caps you're putting on your movement and remove them. You must identify the doors that you have been refusing to walk through, and why. You have to focus on these things, and then do the things that you've never done in order to get to a place where you've never been. This is true for all of your relationships—in business, with your intimate partner, with your family and friends, and even with yourself. In fact, the first relationship you have to tap in to is the relationship you have with yourself, as defined by your spiritual frequency.

Your First Relationship is with You

The biggest challenge in relationships is the feeling we have of being inadequate. (This comes back to the importance of setting the price of our personal value.) Sometimes it shows up in the way we act, like we are superior to or that we must control others. That's all part of fear, which leads you to believe that failing to control the people in your environment will result in pain. You use control as a way to protect yourself. However, it is difficult to give someone a hug with a shield in front of your face. As you lower the shield in front of your own face, you are prepared to show yourself to and be with others.

You master that by staying grounded inside. You do this by remaining present and focusing on one day at a time. When a person reads the Lord's Prayer, it says, "Give us this day". It never says, "Give us a whole week." If you can get through just one day, and you have enough grace and blessing to wake up, then Tuesday will start off just fine. Then you work on Tuesday. Who do you want to be on Tuesday? How do you want to show up on Tuesday? What lessons can you learn from Monday that make you better Tuesday? What lessons can you learn from somebody else on Monday to help you become better Tuesday?

As you live out your life in moments, you are able to accept that you've done your best each day; and when you fall short of the mark, you apologize and keep at it. You accept that you're not perfect and stop expecting perfection. You inherently understand that none of us will ever be perfect, but that we can be perfect within our imperfections. The rest of it is out of your hands, because you can't control what everybody does. You can't fix the world. It is hard enough to fix yourself. You become content to work on yourself, which then prepares you to tap in to a higher frequency within your relationships due to being in a state of learning and growing, as opposed to controlling and fearing. When you release the frequency of fear, you have room for the frequency of love, which is the most powerful frequency of all.

Once I adjusted myself to a higher spiritual frequency and developed the ability to lead with love, opportunities just started naturally coming to me—the same kind of opportunities I'd spent years chasing. Every day, people are showing up in my life who want to play, and they want to play big. People who want to make a huge difference and have the resources to do so. People who are living the dreamer's dream. People I couldn't meet when I was on a low frequency because the wrong person cannot stand to be in the right environment. Even if our paths had crossed, I would not have been equipped with the vision and the frequency to see or to receive them. If you are caught in a perpetual cycle of chasing—chasing people, opportunities, happiness, you name it—then you need to pull back and examine yourself. Finding the right relationship—in money, in business, in intimacy, in life—is not about running faster. It's about reaching higher.

Love

When you hit that highest frequency, the frequency of love, you are able to truly understand and express what love really is. Love is not to love an individual for you, but to love an individual for his or her self. When you love someone for yourself, you constantly experience the disappointment of unmet expectations and a lack that causes you to draw back or react negatively when that person doesn't respond the way you want them to. However, when you have a high spiritual frequency—when you have a mature relationship with yourself—you can live in harmony with every single other human on this planet. If I love you, I love you for you, and I recognize that I don't have the right to have an expectation because you get to be whoever you choose to be. Of course, who you are will determine what my relationship will be with you. I can love you from up close or from across the street. I don't have to have you in my life right now. I don't have to be a part of what you are doing. However, I also don't have to react to what you are doing and get emotional about it.

From that place, you learn how to separate how you really feel from what you know to be true. You move away from the feelings because you realize they can be deceiving. Your relationships will be exponentially improved as you learn not to freak out every time something happens. You are going to learn that you don't have to let outside circumstances dictate how you respond to people you care about in your life. You are going to learn that when things go wrong, you don't have to go wrong with them. You will let go of the fear that others will leave your space, and just rejoice in the time that others spend filling that space with you.

This kind of love shows up in the way you treat people and in the way you communicate. When you talk to people, you are not just speaking to them; you are speaking into them. You are speaking into their nervous system. You are in harmony with them. They cannot just hear you—they can feel you. The way you show up in the lives of other people is going to be one of service. You will always be thinking, "How can I benefit you? How can I enhance what you are doing? How can I be a part of your dream? How can I serve you?" This will cause you to listen more and talk less, and you will listen with intent, instead of just focusing on the next thing you want to say. As you listen this way, other people are going to be drawn to you because you are communicating to them that they are important and that their words matter. You will begin to view your relationships as opportunities to express your desires to their fullest as you serve, instead of viewing the obligation to serve as something that stands in your way to getting where you are trying to go. The needs of others become stepping stones instead of stones obstructing your path.

Love is not just an emotion; it is an attitude. It is not how you feel; it is how you show up. If you show up on a higher level, and you do it consistently repeating the same motions every day, you are going to get specific results, and you are never going to get bored in your relationships. Loving becomes fun, like a game, because there are always new answers to the questions, "How can I make this person even happier? How can I surprise them and put a smile on their face again today?"

I met a 72-year-old gentleman many years ago when I was speaking in Cleveland, Ohio. He specifically came to see me, and we had an opportunity to talk a while. He had on a jogging suit and said he went running every day. He had gold chains down his chest. His hair was dyed black, and it looked natural. He was in great shape. I couldn't believe he was 72. I began to ask him how he kept himself in such great shape, and he said, "I love to work out, but most important, I want to make sure I am around to take care of my family." He said his wife didn't take good care of herself physically and had gained a lot of weight—about 75 pounds. That, in addition to complications with her diabetes, had her in a wheelchair and struggling with several other health challenges as well. He said, "But it doesn't matter. I made a commitment the day I married her that I would love her every single day, and every day I remind myself that's my job. Every day, I declare that I will never, ever disappoint her or go against my word. Every day I love this woman."

That inspired me to the core. At that moment, I had just been through a divorce, and I thought to myself, *I want to be just like him.*

That's the key. It is about getting up, making the decision,. and just staying there. It is about understanding that things change, but you don't have to change within them. And it has to be bigger and more than a person's physical state or how they show up in his or her own life, or in yours. It has to be more than just the things you started off with. It has to be about where you are intentionally going, and how *you* show up. In that way, every relationship you have will add to you and carry you even farther than you could have travelled alone.

Everyone Counts

Everyone who crosses your path is important in your life. Everyone you ever meet is going to be a great example of what you can become, or a reminder of what you no longer want to be. They all count. Some are going to show you new paths, and you are going to see things in them that you can aspire to be. You learn to emulate what you see, to duplicate that, and make it your own. Others will show you what you never want to be and why. You will learn to consciously avoid them in order to keep yourself from falling into the trappings of being a victim or a low-frequency person. When you start operating that way, you are going to develop a higher frequency of gratitude in all of your relationships because you will recognize how each person in your life is a custom fit for something you need to learn or to remember.

You will be that person for others, too. Whatever choices you make, you affect other people and the very layout of the universe. We each impact others around us whether we want to or not. When one thing happens, something else happens. There's an ancient saying that says, "When you find your soulmate, be kind to him and love him because your meeting, your union, took thousands of years to create and to manifest."

Each of us have a work to do, and each of us is here to make a difference. We are all connected, and we all matter. Every deposit we make into the world and into our relationships creates a ripple in the universe. For example, I got involved in an organization in 1994, and I worked closely with one of the leaders. He was a young gentleman, thirteen years younger than I, who had set in motion a chain of events that brought me into that group. He had enrolled another gentleman, who enrolled another gentleman, who enrolled another young lady, who enrolled another gentleman, who then enrolled me. I look back on everything that has happened in my life since I joined that group. If I hadn't made that decision in 1994, as a result of other people's ripples, I would not even be writing this book right now. I would not have met the woman that I married and have a son with. I would not have had the next opportunity that opened so many important doors that led me to where I am today. I would not have had so many of the experiences I have had. Everything in my life would have shifted, had that young man who was thirteen years younger than me not decided to join an organization and to work hard at it. Sure, I may have ended up in the organization anyway, but it would have been with different people, with a different type of understanding, and with different experiences. Everything would have been on a different course because I would have been riding the wave of a different ripple and been in different locations. If I had been in different locations, I could not have been where I needed to be to meet the people in my life that have impacted my life in the most profound ways.

We affect each other. We are all connected. We always have been. We forever will be. How are you affecting others? What kinds of ripples are you making?

The quality of the ripples you initiate will be determined by your attitude. Your attitude is an additive energy that affects others based on the frequency you're broadcasting. An "additive" is like a flavor extract or extra energy coming from you that directly impacts the environment of the people around you. You must always remember that your presence within each of your relationships is always creating and is never stagnant. You want to be intentional with that creative power, always making sure that it is restorative in nature by adding value and substance to another person's environment. Be conscious of pushing others to new heights, and be consistent in doing so. Always strive to be a value creator. Let that become your mantra. Talk yourself into this, living that way every single day until it becomes natural to you. "I am a value creator. I create value everywhere I go. In each relationship, if I don't create value, I shouldn't be in that relationship."

It is about what you come to give, not what you get in return. When you live in that frequency, you are going to get it all anyway because you gave it all. You are going to have abundance because you gave your time, your energy, and your service all from your soul. That is the frequency of abundance; so when you live from that place, abundance will naturally find its way to you. Just as frequencies are always in search of like frequencies.

Love is a Verb

By definition, a frequency is always moving, and each frequency has its own unique pattern of movement. A higher frequency will require more movement and action in order for you to stay there. Because love is the highest frequency there is, it will require the most action. Love is a verb. You can't just plug in, lay back on the couch, close your eyes, and be on automatic pilot. Love is an action emotion, an action power, and an action energy. If you stop moving, you will sink into a different, less desirable frequency in which the relationship will not be nourished. Unfortunately, it is commonplace for people to be in a relationship and not have goals on why they are there. They haven't agreed on a destination together, believing that the relationship itself is the destination. This means that as soon as they are there and say, "I love you," they stop moving because they have arrived. The relationship quickly becomes stagnant, and neither party is growing. Soon, the relationship falls apart because there is no such thing as standing still. If you're not moving forward, you are moving backward.

The things that last are the things that are moving forward. Happiness is the byproduct of growth—of things being manifested and created. However, it doesn't mean you have to exhaust yourself. If you bring yourself into harmony with this higher frequency, you can tap in to the flow of its current and move along with it. You will be moving and doing more than you've ever had to do at lower frequencies, but you will no longer be pushing, so it will feel easier and more natural.

I can tell you from experience that being in the same line of frequency with another person, whether naturally or because you both made the conscious decision to tune into that same channel and live there—it just doesn't get any better than that. My wife and I have shared goals and dreams, even as we maintain individual goals and dreams. I know what she wants, and she knows what I want.

We know what we want together. We use our relationship as a vehicle to achieve what we're looking for as a couple, and what we're looking for as individuals. We are in a constant process of discovery and growth, separately and together. When two people are working in two separate spheres, whether they have two different experiences in the same workplace or are working in two entirely different industries, it may first appear that nothing is in alignment between them. However, they can then come together and have common goals of why they are together. What are we trying to achieve? What do we want to do? What kind of family are we trying to raise? What kind of example do we want to set? What type of story are we trying to tell? How can we help to bless the world and empower others through our story and our mistakes, good and bad? When you have that, it doesn't matter where your separate spheres exist. When I walk in from my day and my wife walks in from her day, we have something to talk about. We are back in alignment again. We are back in alignment with the vibration that lives in our house and, more important, in our relationship.

You will have to maintain that frequency on purpose by keeping open channels of communication. It's important to be able to let out however you feel because clutter blocks vibrations. The level of your success in every aspect of your life is contingent on your ability to effectively communicate, whether verbally, through your energy, or non-verbally, through your actions. You don't have to respond to every transgression, but you must commit to have honest, open communication when you do respond. You must always share respectfully and speak out of love. Sharing your feelings never requires that you hurt other people or tear them down and make them feel like they are less than. If a person runs into guilt or shame, it doesn't help them become better—it helps them become worse because humans tend to act out when messages such as, "I'm not good enough. I don't deserve love. I'm not worthy enough, or smart enough," shows up in their emotions. When they internalize that message, they live it out. You can see examples of this as you look back at the low-level frequency relationships you've had, and maybe even in your own history. If, instead, you can create a relationship with open channels of positive, honest communication, the vibration will be so high that it will be a place where each of you will be fed and fully charged.

The bottom line is that, ideally, your relationships will always foster partnerships. This takes action and setting your frequency with intention. As you set your frequency, you will attract others who are on that same frequency into relationships with you—in business, in your intimate partnership, and in all areas of your life. Will you be perfect? No, and don't beat yourself up when you fall short. We are not perfect, but we don't have to be. However, as you commit to taking the action that perfect love demands, you will naturally raise your frequency. This is not something that can happen overnight, but you want to strive for it each and every day because it feels so good. Each day, wake up with a renewed commitment to be present in your relationships and to love a little bit more than you did the day before. Commit first to adjust your paradigm and the way that you think, which will naturally transform the way you live. What you live, you learn. What you learn, you practice. What you practice, you become.

CHAPTER TEN
The Law of Agreement

The Law of Agreement is at the basis of all life and is the energy that leads to transformation and expansion. I am discussing it first in the context of the frequency of relationships, but it is relevant to all frequencies, and indeed is the magnifier of every frequency. For instance, if you look at the transformation that takes place at conception, it's a matter of cells dividing into more. More of what? More of the same. In order for cells to mirror each other, they have to have proper communication, which is simply the transfer or exchange of information. In order for this information to be exchanged—sent out and then received—there must be agreement. A cell produces more of what it needs by birthing its own self into existence. Now there is more of what it is, all heading toward a desired destiny. This is what's needed for all of life to continue to perpetuate.

If you subscribe to the Biblical account of creation, you will recall that in the beginning God created the heavens and the earth. The rest of the account is a series of things being divided and pushed into more—all things giving birth after its own kind. There was only a single point of creation, after which life extended from a series of divisions and births, which is essentially multiplication.

The point here is that in order to transform into more, you must have agreement. Agreement is the foundation for transformation. In relationships, where you begin with others determines your end results. Both personally and in business, agreement is at the core of all successful relationships. As you can see, the basis of universal growth and expansion is found in how you exchange, and then what extends thereafter from your exchanges. All of existence is a succession of relationships or exchanges that advance life into continuous new existences, whether positive or negative.

The 12 Energies of Agreement

If you enter into relationships based on your purpose and destiny, then those relationships will magnify your efforts to fulfill them. Where there's a group of people in agreement turned towards the destiny of one's dream, the dream will undoubtedly manifest. Once the biological, energetic, and scientific demands are met for that environment, the resulting transformations become just a formality. **All energy that is properly balanced leads to absolute results.**

In order to properly balance the energy of your agreements, you need to recognize the twelve energies that comprise all agreements. Every human is genetically designed to respond to these twelve frequencies, as they trigger different biological processes in your body in the form of emotions. Emotions are strong motivators to the way that you move through your life. This is not by accident, but by design. Every feeling you have serves a spiritual purpose, but is fundamentally a biological hormonal state caused by the movement and placement of neurotransmitters in the body, which then influence the physiology of the individual. The presence or absence of any of the twelve energies of agreement in your exchanges with another person will trigger an emotional response, therefore causing movement of the hormones and neurotransmitters in the person's body receiving (or not receiving) attention. In essence, you are an artist transforming each person you come in contact with, or you are a canvas being transformed.

I am going to share with you some quick definitions and purposes of each component, followed by how to actualize that energy in your personal relationships, and examples of how to apply that energy in a meeting with a prospective business relationship. Pay close attention to how each component makes a person feel. Learn all twelve until they become an inseparable part of your conscience.

1. **Attention:** Attention is the greatest contribution of oneself that can be offered. Attention received is how one knows that he or she is alive.

    Makes you and others feel: special.

    Personal: You must make sure you're getting the attention you need.

    Business: Give immediate attention based on what you become aware of, and then serve in some type of way. "Let me get you some coffee. Let me get your coat."

2. **Awareness**: Be aware of a person's condition. Speak towards what you are aware of. It can be a person's birthday, something about themselves that they may have spoken of at an earlier time, or a particular need. Be active towards what you are aware of.

    Makes you and others feel: thought of.

    Personal: You do not need those around you who remain unaware of your specialness.

    Business: Beyond offering to serve a client's need, hear what is being said by the client and note it, then at later points in the conversation, repeat back what you heard. This shows that you are well aware of their concerns.

3. **Accommodation**: Be accommodating at all times. Accommodation forces comfort. It is one of the most valuable parts of service.

    Makes you and others feel: comfortable.

    Personal: People should be accommodating towards you to reduce stress or the weight of your activity.

Business: If the client has a scheduling conflict for your meeting, be flexible with your own schedule to accommodate a time that is most convenient for the client.

4. **Adoration**: Always notice what's good about an individual and be ready to speak towards that.

    Makes you and others feel: worthy.

    Personal: Those who you are in a relationship with should always speak right things into you.

    Business: Use positive compliments as an introduction.

5. **Absolution**: When you speak your word, follow up on your word. Integrity builds confidence with both parties. Only make commitments and decisions that you can follow up on.

    Makes you and others feel: trusting.

    Personal: People should keep their word when they make a commitment to you.

    Business: In offering your product or services, you must be decisive.

6. **Availability**: Be sure to prioritize the needs of others. Present yourself for availability.

    Makes you and others feel: connected.

    Personal: Sometimes you need to be prioritized.

    Business: Beyond the point of your meeting or engagement, open yourself to being available by phone or email.

7. **Acceleration**: The role that you play in the life of another should always produce results at a recognizable pace. Never be slow about producing results. Be quick to solve a problem. Answer concerns promptly.

    Makes you and others feel: valued and supported.

    Personal: When people make commitments towards you, they should not drag their feet.

    Business: Be conscious of the pace your product or service produces results.

8. **Access**: Be inviting. Open your space. Never allow people to feel distance.
   Makes you and others feel: welcomed and accepted.
   Personal: Doors should be open to you.
   Business: If you're using a space or display space, invite people in.

9. **Acknowledgement**: Notice points of greatness, then tell that greatness to a third party. Edify.
   Makes you and others feel: promoted.
   Personal: You should get credit for your actions.
   Business: If a third person is present, make compliments to the third party about something you noticed or heard about your potential client or customer.

10. **Authentication**: Always surround yourself with those who know more than you. Also, share your advanced knowledge to improve the life of someone else.
    Makes you and others feel: exalted.
    Personal: Associate with those who know more than you and who can push your efforts.
    Business: Have some process of authentication ready to go at all times.

11. **Action**: Always present sufficient action and present efficient action towards others that is affective and effective.
    Makes you and others feel: engaged.
    Personal: Align with those who will be willing to participate in your ideas.
    Business: Take action towards something that is not a part of the sale or client acquisition, such as: "Well in the meantime while you are considering..., I'll go ahead and do...for you."

12. **Accountability**: Hold yourself accountable in all exchanges.
    Makes you and others feel: secure.

Personal: People should hold themselves accountable towards your dreams as well as theirs.

Business: Identify three or more points of future contact with your client to measure or assess satisfaction.

Practicing these twelve energies or laws of agreement will bring exacting results. Each of these twelve components have their own frequency, and they all work together to create synergy toward a common purpose. As you activate each of these behaviors towards a person, it plants in them a feeling. People do not necessarily have to believe in your idea, but they must believe in you. When you take time to invest a series of feelings, this causes them to align with the energy of your body. The frequencies you broadcast literally affect the hormones and neurotransmitters of the other person, which creates and forces new biological cycles within them—cycles that build or regenerate productive energy. All cycles as they intertwine with other cycles produce new cycles. Cycles both require and perpetuate agreement.

For example, let's consider how these agreements apply to your business relationships, as demonstrated above. Instead of making sales, create agreements. Your concentration should never be on the sale or signing up a new client, but should be focused towards the creation of a relationship stemming from agreement and its twelve laws or energies. This is equally true for obtaining long-term clients or presenting an opportunity for someone to make a purchase from you. By emanating these qualities of agreement, your client or customer will find themselves in your world where an exchange removes itself from being an object of question to being an object of desire. When a person aligns with you in agreement by the investments you make in them, the product, or service becomes inconsequential—they have already bought into *you*.

As you build a community around you of people who have these natural lines of agreement with you, you will have a blank canvas ready for your expression. Whenever you express a desire, your spirit transforms into an information mechanism that is readily shared with your circle. In the root of the word *information* is the word *form*. The word "inform" denotes that there is a catalyst to what is formed. Your spirit literally becomes the center of creation. When you express a desire within your community, you are immediately supported. However, you must take it upon yourself to build relationships based on the twelve agreements for this type of magic to happen.

Often, when things are not happening for you, things are not getting done, or experiences do not end up as expected, you can trace it back to the people around you. Use these twelve energies of agreement to measure the value of your relationships, and recalibrate as needed. Everything between you and others in your circle must be aligned according to the Law of Agreement. The damage that is caused to you when it is not may be subtle, but it will interrupt your connection to your own spirit. When that connection is interrupted, your adjoining connections are interrupted as well. In essence, without these twelve energies being fed, your spirit can be left broken. The one thing you want to make sure that you have is a vibrant spirit. When the frequency of your spirit is prioritized, you will always have the power to facilitate the seeds of your dreams, and a well facilitated seed will guarantee the transformation and abundance you're looking for.

Feelings that stem from Agreement

- Attention— A person feels special.
- Awareness – A person feels thought of.
- Accommodation – A person feels comforted.
- Adoration – A person feels worthy.
- Absolution – A person feels trusting.
- Availability – A person feels connected.

- Acceleration – A person feels supported.
- Access – A person feels accepted.
- Acknowledgement – A person feels promoted.
- Authentication – A person feels exalted.
- Action – A person feels engaged.
- Accountability – A person feels secure.

CHAPTER ELEVEN
The Frequency of Finance

Today more than ever, people are trying to find new ways to make money, to earn a living, and to take care of their families. The world has changed dramatically. Manufacturing jobs have moved from the United States to countries where there are lower tax liabilities, lower costs of production, and lower wages. Recessions and job loss are common. The future of the Social Security Trust Funds is uncertain, and people worry about losing the savings and the security they have spent years accumulating and counting on.

The outlook seems grim, and the outcry is discouraging.

Luckily, there are two sides to every coin, and the flip side of this one is bright and full of hope. When you think about it, the world is changing so fast because of technology, which isn't a bad thing. With this technology and ingenuity comes the opportunity for money to be created faster than ever before. The amount of time it takes to conceive of an idea and bring it to market is becoming smaller and smaller with the utilization of the Internet and your access to the global economy.

However, even aside from all of that, your ability to create financial abundance in your life is independent of the current economy. Your financial wealth is simply a reflection of the financial frequency on which you reside. If you are on a low frequency, you will not be able to recognize or take advantage of the opportunities as they present themselves. You will not be able to trade the potential for wealth into actual dollars. The true doorway to your abundance is not opportunity, but an abundant mindset and frequency so that you can recognize and take advantage of the infinite number of opportunities that already surround you. All you have to do is tap in to an abundant frequency.

Remember, frequency is energy. Money is energy. And energy cannot be destroyed or created—just transferred. Money energy is an exchange. That's all it is, and everyone can participate. You may wonder why some people attract money easily when other people work twelve-hour days and can barely make ends meet. This is simply a reflection of the difference in their financial frequencies they are sending out. You create these frequencies with your thoughts, feelings, and consciousness.

Many are living under the *illusion* of money. Money is not money the way you're used to thinking about it. It is not a number that is in your bank account, or the sum of what you want it be, or even what you dream of exchanging it for. True money runs at a higher frequency than most participate in. Most Americans live in lower frequencies of exchange and cannot perceive this truth. Therefore, they feel that those who live at the highest frequency of exchange should put aside money and give it to the lower frequency participants. In reality, this would be a futile effort. It wouldn't change anything because those who live and exchange at lower frequencies would only squander the money at the frequency in which they live. You can see this with lottery winners who win millions of dollars and then are right back at the poverty level where they started within three to five years. This is because your idea of money is not based in fact, or what is possible. It runs on a frequency and is congruent to where you are.

The Five Monkeys

Financial frequencies are often locked in generationally by the things your family talked about at the dinner table. If your family was at a low financial frequency, it probably began when someone decided not to aim too high in order to avoid the humiliation and pain that comes from failure. Those attitudes shaped behaviors and interpretations, which were then passed down from generation to generation.

Consider the fable of the five monkeys. In this story, researchers conduct an experiment with five monkeys in a pen with a ladder leading up to a bunch of bananas. The first monkey approaches the ladder and starts to climb, but is then sprayed with a fire hose. Every time a monkey goes up to get a banana, the conductor of the experiment sprays him with water and knocks him back down. One by one, the hungry monkeys try to retrieve the bananas, but the water keeps them for succeeding. Eventually, any time a monkey proceeds to climb, the group reacts by pulling him down off the ladder to keep him from being sprayed. Then, one monkey is removed from the pen and replaced with a new monkey who has never been sprayed. The new monkey quite naturally sees the bananas and tries to go up the ladder. The other four monkeys attack him and pull him down until he learns not to try anymore. Then the conductors remove another monkey from the pen and replace him with another new monkey who has never been sprayed. Again, the newcomer tries to go up the ladder. This time, not only do the three native monkeys pull him down, but the first newcomer who had never been sprayed also joins in the attack. The pattern of replacement continues until all five monkeys in the pen are monkeys who have never been sprayed, and who maintain the same pattern of behavior and response to the bananas. Not only do they avoid climbing the ladder, but they are united in their response to attacking any monkey who tries. The behavior and response is locked in.

If you aren't getting the results you want, you are simply locked into a frequency that is not aligned with those results. What you think, believe, and act out in your financial life sends out an energy and frequency that attracts itself to a like frequency. Each frequency is an entire world of being and experience. Going from one frequency to another is like stepping into an alternate reality. For instance, if you're listening to the radio at an FM station, it's as if the AM frequency doesn't exist. They don't share space, as they are in two entirely different spaces. Similarly, you are only going to get what you are tapped in to financially. Historically, you can see this transformation in the early modern human as he matures from one frequency to the other, or from one understanding to a new understanding. He takes the idea of growing his sustenance near his home versus hunting for it. Now his time is better spent with greater accumulation. The same has to happen today. If you have little money, you cannot simply go out and work for more money to get it. For an abundant yield, you must venture to a higher understanding of how money works. You have to move to the frequency of greater accumulation. To do this, you must first attack your lack, or your lack will attack you.

Attack Your Lack

You must eliminate the negative language you use to communicate about money. I mean this in every sense, both verbally and nonverbally. Shift the way that you think, speak, and act about money. Our emotions and thoughts are all made of energy and have a frequency. They combine together to create a powerful current that moves us toward the object of their attention. Most people think about money in terms of worry. The foundation of their relationship with money is based on lack, which defines the way they think about and live out their relationship with money. They are looking to pay a bill, need to buy a new car, or have to get an automobile fixed. They have loans, or they are on a fixed income. Their whole focus and energy is projected towards not having enough instead of being focused towards abundance. When you are focused on the holes in your finances, that is where you are going to show up, and that is where you are going to live. You are what your predominant thoughts are.

When you ride down the road and you see a car that lost control and hit a pole, notice that the poles are usually several yards away from each other—plenty of space apart for a car to go in between. So, then, why do people hit the pole? It's because they are staring at that pole while they are losing control, hoping they don't hit it. The frequency they are sending out is, "Pole! Pole! Pole!" In their conscious mind, they are attracting that pole by sending their life force and frequency toward it. In their effort to avoid it, they are in actuality focusing on the pole, and therefore increasing the likelihood they will hit it. This is why in race-car driving, the drivers are trained to do the opposite. They are told that if you lose control of the car, never look at the wall; always look at the grass. You always look where you want the car to go because that's where your focus is. This is true in life. Even in that state where you are losing control and you know that something bad can happen, if you focus your attention, your thoughts, and your frequency towards a solution, then the solution is going to be more accessible to you.

This is why it is so important to have a big, magnificent vision of where you want your life to be, instead of just focusing on the place you feel stuck right now. Where do you really want to go? How do you really want to live? Start thinking about what you want instead of what you don't want. Stephen Covey said that you must begin with the end in mind. You ought to be able to see the end while you are in the middle of the journey. Know what it looks like. If you hit a wall and something is not what you thought it would be, you simply reroute and continue toward the same destination. It pulls you. You naturally move along with the flow of energy.

The Law of Expectancy

This demonstrates the Law of Expectancy. You are living out the law of expectancy in your life right now. Whatever you expect is what you manifest. If you expect a lack, there will be a lack. Likewise, if you make a shift and expect to win, you will. I have never met a winner that didn't first expect to win. The achiever is always looking for ways to become resourceful and is always looking for opportunities. The intelligent, smart, and wise achievers are always getting ready for success way before it comes because they know they are on course to receive it. They are simply waiting for the gap to close. They know that success is the point where opportunity meets preparedness. People who are always preparing themselves for something better have a different level of expectancy. When the time comes and the window is open, they are already poised to jump out of it.

To be in alignment with the frequency of positive expectancy, you have to show up a certain way. When people are down and out, they feel down and out. They feel like they are lacking in life, and they can't pay their bills. There is a low energy and frequency of helplessness, fear, and a lack of control. To live in the frequency of positive expectancy demands that you take back that control. Otherwise, you will stay at a low frequency, which is going to attract more lack into your life.

Remember, frequencies are always in alignment. The Universe will give you more of what it is that you declare. If you are at a frequency of one hundred percent broke, you are going to tune in to that frequency, and that's what you are going to receive. If you have a frequency of *I just need enough*, then that's the frequency that you are going to receive. If you proclaim that you expect a frequency of abundance, that you deserve and desire it, and you are willing to work for it, have the behaviors to follow it up, and that this is going to be part of your life and part of the very essence of who you are, then the abundance is bound to come. Even if you don't have two cents right now, your course is set, and it's just a matter of time before the gap is going to close.

Shift Your Money Mindset

In 1992, I had just sold all my businesses and left Chicago to move to Atlanta. I was starting my life all over again. One day, I was sitting with a friend whom I had a lot of respect for because he was always calm, positive, knew how to have a lot of fun, and he lived very well. He had the best parties, drank the best wines, lived in the best homes, and wore the best clothes. At the time, I had a new idea for a business I wanted to run by him. I said, "Look man, I have a great idea, and I am going to make a million dollars."

He looked at me and said, "Just one?"

I felt like I was two inches tall. Since that day, I have never thought so small again. When I make my goals, I make them humongous goals. When people say they want to make a million dollars in their lifetime, I say I want to make $250 million in three years.

Honestly, it's not about the money. It's about the capacity to exchange for the things I most desire for me and my family. Abundance gives me the opportunity to give back and to make a difference in the lives of other people. If you don't have freedom from money and get out of the constraints of lack, then you are limited in what you can have and what you can give because most of your time is spent working. Everywhere you look, you see people who make a lot of money but who don't have a lot of time, and people who have a lot of time but don't have a lot of money. The balance lies in stepping into a new understanding of exchange and receiving. Accept and embrace the fact that as a human being, you are part of the community of the world. You have a mighty work to do and you have unlimited resources to get it done. It is not just your right, but it is your responsibility to walk in abundance—the abundance that is there for all of mankind. When we live in this state of abundance, our vibrational energy will precede us. It will go out as our representative, claiming the increase your frequency demands.

As you align yourself with higher frequencies in the other areas of your life, you will more easily rise out of the lack mentality. However, the reverse is also true. The more chronically you rest at lower frequencies in other areas of your life, the greater the pull will be to stay in your lack mentality. Your abundance is a manifestation of what is happening on all of your other frequencies.

- **The frequency of your relationships**: When you speak of money, you speak of value, which is based upon the agreement between two people. You have to set your value in order for others to come into agreement with that value in order for there to be a basis for exchange.

- **Spiritual frequency**: Money is an energy and comes from the dream-seeds you plant in your spirit.
- **Physical frequency**: Your abundance is tied to the amount of energy you are able to invest into performance. The proper performance will bring you a more abundant lifestyle financially. Staying at a low physical frequency cripples your earning potential.
- **Frequency of your mindset**: The money you are able to receive is in direct correlation to your mindset about money and abundance.

All of the five frequencies feed into each other, so it is difficult to label the end and the beginning to the process of raising your financial frequency. However, in order to make a change, you have to shift away from the lack mindset and realize that there is in fact no lack in the world. There is more than enough for everyone. This isn't just true about the dollars and cents in the world, but about what we equate to money—sustenance and abundance. Think about it. The birds will never starve, there is always enough carbon for the trees to grow, and there is always going to be enough moisture in our ecosystem to sustain life. The universe is able to take care of itself. It is able to take care of you. When you have this heightened mental frequency and mindset, you will see endless opportunities instead of endless lack. You will naturally look for ways to be creative, to create more value, to be able to bring things to the marketplace.

If you want to have abundance in your financial life, you must understand that energy is magnetic. It attracts experiences to match wherever we are. Life doesn't just happen. You have to accept and embrace the fact that there is abundance that resides in you and the frequency of that abundance is accessible to you, right now.

Most people don't receive their blessings or the rewards of the way that they live because they don't believe that they are good enough to receive them. Remove those blocks. Let them fall at your feet and breathe, with your arms open wide to receive everything coming your way. Understand that everything in the universe is there at your disposal. Visualize everything in the universe is pouring into your bank accounts, your mind, your spirit, and your relationships.

Hope and Gratitude

The second step toward raising your financial frequency is taking a deep-sea dive into hope and gratitude for the abundance you receive, even before it happens. Everything in life happens two times. The thought and the thing; the spiritual and the physical; the inner and the outer.

When I lived in Atlanta, Georgia, I went through some tough times and ended up being homeless. I might have been able to get bailed out, but my pride wouldn't let me. I wanted to fight through it. I wanted to grow up and to take responsibility. I knew there was another way. Four years earlier, someone whom I respected shared with me his story about what he had gone through to get where he was. I understood the words of Abraham Lincoln when he said, "If one person can, another person can." In hearing his story, I began to stay the course in the middle of the mess. It gave me hope.

Hope is one of the greatest fuels—a premium gasoline—for raising your frequency because it dramatically changes your perception of the world. They did an experiment with six mice in which they put the mice in a bin filled with water. They put a lid on top of the bin so that the mice were in complete darkness. Within the first seven minutes, all of the mice had drowned. Then they put more mice in the bin of water, but this time they kept the cover open enough to allow a little hole of light. The mice swam around for six hours. When you have hope, there is also going to be endurance and a greater life force. This will dramatically change your view of where you're going. When you change the way you look at things, the things you look at begin to change.

When my life began to fall apart, I was sleeping in a car in the parking lot of a hotel and pulling a comforter over my head with a smile on my face because I was looking into my future, and it was magnificent. I knew I was going to be wealthy because my hope illuminated the reality of that future. I could see it so clearly. I began to continue to be positive when everything around me seemed to be negative. I began to be the oddball in the negative circumstance. I didn't fit in there anymore. If you don't fit in there, it is going to spit you out. I spent my time around the people who had the frequency I wanted to match. I read the books that fed my hope. I did everything in my power to close the gap between where I was and where I knew I was going to be.

How would your life change if you embraced this same sense of certainty and hope? If you walked out your door with a sense of expectancy, even if you just have two nickels in your pocket? If you walked and talked as if you were abundant, and if you treated people with the understanding that your place in the world is to give, not just to take, and that everything will be provided for you? Every day when you wake up in the morning, declare your intentions:

Today, I accept that the Universe has something great for me. I expect this, and I am preparing myself for these gifts. I am willing to pay the price because I know it is worthwhile, and I know it is necessary. I know my family is dependent upon me to be able to provide and to perform at a higher level each and every day. I am now in alignment with my financial frequency of abundance—the frequency that is my birthright. This abundance allows me to do good in the world. I am a great example for those who follow me, who listen to my words, and who see my deeds. I live it. I accept it. I acknowledge that it is mine, and I am thankful and humble.

I am grateful each and every day for those things that are coming to me, even though they are not yet here. I know they are coming, and I can see them even,

though my eyes are closed. I can see them even though they are not in my hands.
They are still mine.

They are coming.

They are coming.

As you make your declaration each day, it will begin to reprogram your subconscious mind with this sense of acceptance. This will change the way you show up in the world. You will open avenues of new energy—new actions—that will create a new current in your life to take you in a new direction. You will be drawn towards and interested in the things that will be in alignment with what you most want and *expect* for your life. You are going to start to read and study your craft. You are going to start going to empowering events. You are going to start looking for people who play at a high level, who are very successful, and who are giving back to the world. You will begin to immerse yourself and start to live in that space, even if you don't have two nickels in your bank account today. You are going to live life as though you were already there, and then you are going to accept the fact that you attract it easily because that's part of who you are. That's going to help you take massive action, and when you take that action, that action is going to yield results. As you take action to move beyond the fear that has chained you to lower levels of frequency, the Universe will make room for you and the world will come and kneel at your feet and offer up its riches to you.

CHAPTER TWELVE
Ideas and Action

You are either going to work in harmony with abundance, or it will work in harmony against you because it does not compromise. It is not enough to think in terms of abundance. You must act in terms of abundance. Changing your frequency is not a spectator sport. You act as if. So, the key is to find out how to tap in to the actions that will allow you to work in harmony with the frequency of abundance.

When you fail to act, you become a victim. Victims do not act because they are drowning in being acted upon. When you operate as a victim, that's one of the lowest centers of energy. Victims blame their results on somebody else because they can't bare the possibility that they have the power to change their circumstances. "You have the power to change," is misinterpreted by victims as, "It's your fault," and "You're not good enough." When people feel like they can't do it, they stop trying. They become dead fish going with the flow of their reality. Being a conscious creator requires action.

You are what you think, but you will lose what you think if you do not put the proper energy, or action, behind it. The thoughts, emotions, and beliefs required to stay in the frequency of abundance both produce and are the result of specific behavior. What actions will move you into the space of the frequency of financial abundance? To answer this, you must understand the value of imagination and ideas. Throughout Earth's history, you will find that people who had the greatest imagination and the greatest ideas garnered more money than others, or garnered more material to serve as a medium for exchange. To understand this better, let's look at the birth of imagination and ideas.

Idea + Energy = Increase

Energy is what it takes to bring an idea into experience. Another word for energy is work. It takes work to turn an idea into currency. The better the idea, along with consistent work, the greater the currency that can be used as a medium of exchange. However, without the work, it will come to nothing. Most people have great ideas, but they don't feed them, so they die. Every shift or transformation you have ever experienced is the result of taking action. Every lost opportunity is the result of inaction.

I remember watching Les Brown on PBS more than twenty years ago. I was inspired by his presence, and I wanted to be a speaker like him. I thought to myself, *I have the gift of gab, and I have something to say. I can always talk and make people laugh and draw people in. I could do that.* As soon as the desire was born in me, there were other voices in my head that crowded it out. *I don't know how. I can run restaurants better than anyone, but speaking like that should be left to those who have a formal education. I don't have the right words. I'm not good enough.* I validated those beliefs by acting like I didn't care. I chose to believe I had missed the opportunity instead of recognizing that my desire itself was proof of the opportunity. I was not in an abundant mindset. I believed only one person could do what Les had done. There wasn't room for me at the top. So, I went into a frequency that brought me even lower because I started to play the victim. My negative response to possibility moved me down from my naturally positive personality to a place where now I played the victim to my lack of education. I didn't know then that he didn't have an education either. I just saw the power and the passion with which he was speaking, and I was intimidated.

However, I couldn't stay in that frequency. The idea kept coming back to me, burning a little more each time. Because I *did* care.

I allowed my caring to grow into a drive that pushed me to take the necessary actions to close the gap between where I was and where I wanted to be. Now, Les and I have been great friends for the last twenty years. We feed off of each other, and I still learn a tremendous amount from him through his example—the way he treats his children, and the way he inspires himself and keeps other people inspired. Even though he might be having challenges with his health or in other aspects of his life, when he shows up, he shows up big. I have the privilege of witnessing and participating in his greatness. I am grateful I found the courage to carve out my way to this place. The first step was changing my thought patterns, but if I hadn't taken the initiative to start stepping in that direction, I never would have been able to fully move out of my state of low frequency and into a more lucrative frequency.

The History of Man

Let's take a closer look at how this pattern of action has worked hand in hand with abundance throughout the history of mankind. In the early stages of the modern human, hunting was the primary basis of work to obtain food sustenance. Food included both vegetation and meat. In order for a family to eat, one had to go out and hunt for food and then bring that food back to the homestead. One day, someone had a revolutionary idea for providing nutritional essentials for the family. Let's take corn, for example. A man goes out and spends a considerable amount of time looking for corn. Once he finds it, he pulls the stocks off the branches, puts them in a carrying case, and brings them home.

One day he takes the time to ask the question, "How does this corn grow?" Upon finding out the source of the corn, which is the seed, he realizes if he brings the seed home and plants the seed, the corn will then be next to the house and will therefore save him the time it takes to go out and hunt for it. From this, later lessons were discovered: You can put aside seed every year in anticipation of supplying the family with enough corn to last the season. Subsequently, he realizes that he can grow more corn than he needs for any one season, leaving extra corn. Here you see the birth of an economy, because now he can supply another family that has less or no corn. He can offer the corn in exchange for something else he needs.

The energy that was spent on gathering is now spent growing, harvesting, and exchanging. This idea was applied to all food sources, including meat. You grow the food close to home versus going out to hunt and bringing maybe just one kill home to feed the family. The energy that was once spent obtaining one item of sustenance can now be used to procure many. A greater yield without greater effort. In essence, he was able to meet his other needs for free because the surplus was grown with the same energy that it took to hunt.

This early move from being mere survivors to being creators is a prime example of the relationship between ideas and energy. It is also the foundation for what money is—an exchange. When you add action to an idea or a concept, it becomes manifest. It is one door leading to many doors. The person who can do this the best garners the most currency.

Ask Questions

Note that the inception of the idea came as a result of a question: How does this corn grow? Asking questions—better questions— will guide you in the creation of new ideas. A question directs the energy of your thoughts and moves you from one space into the next. If you want better outcomes, ask better questions. Here are several that will help to initiate your transformation and perpetuate the seeds of new ideas. I recommend taking the time to write out your answers to each and every one of these. Action begets action.

- What can I do differently today to help me master financial abundance in my life?
- What can I exchange?
- What service can I offer?
- How can I serve the world?
- What value can I create that will bring that abundance back to me tenfold?
- Where can I find the people who can inspire me, help me, guide me, or even coach me?
- How do I create value for those people so that they will let me into their lives?
- How do I create value for the world?
- What is my big vision, or my big goal?
- What must I do to become better this day?
- What books and videos will bring closer to my goal and the understanding I need?
- What are the needs of others that I am uniquely qualified to fill?

Money and Truth

Looking again at this scenario of early man, you will recognize that his ideas opened his life so that there was more space to exchange, which benefited both himself and those with whom he was exchanging. As he exercised the manifestation of his idea, doing so led to greater and greater opportunities and ways to serve his purpose and receive more of what he wanted, which was to provide more efficiently for he and his family. The nature of this truth is important to note, which is this: the idea served *his* greater purposes and desires, and then as he allowed that idea to serve him, he was able to serve others with his surplus. First himself, and then, by extension of his needs being met fully and thoroughly, the others who he was appointed to serve. The highest frequency of abundance follows this same pattern.

Your pursuit of money will fall within one of two categories:

1. Life-support system
2. Lie-Support system

Money equals truth. Money can equal your truth, or it can equal someone else's. It is inevitable that you are what you think, so you must take into consideration the source of your thinking. A lot of what people do in terms of what happens in their brain is not thinking. Remember, it takes energy to push and to develop an idea. Energy equals work. Energy is determined by the action you take. To determine your truth, you must determine the direction your energy is pointed. However, when we think of money and how to increase our abundance, our energy is often spent developing someone else's idea. This can never lead to true wealth because it interrupts the natural pattern and nature of true abundance.

Consider the wealthy families in America who have long histories of wealth. These are families such as J. P. Morgan, the Rothschilds, the Rockefellers and others who found long-lasting wealth. Most people view these wealthy people, who are at the top one percent of the American wealth system, with disdain, as if they do not have the right to be wealthy. In truth, most of their wealth was built by a great-great grandfather, or even older generationally. Those first men started with a small idea, and, through work, moved the idea towards accomplishment. By doing so, they secured wealth for many generations. Because of their surplus, they had a medium of exchange. Their ideas became a life-support system.

On the other hand, consider the people who labored to build the empires of those men. Their ideas sent out a beacon to those who were in agreement with their dreams and terms of exchange. People came to support the manifestation of the visions of these men. Laborers, foremen, accountants, strategists—the worker bees necessary to move the idea through the ranks of accomplishment. The worker bees—what came of their wealth and their legacy? Of course, they received monetary compensation for their contributions as agreed based on the terms of the exchange. However, when your energy is spent building the wealth of another, you cannot quite depend on that to secure your own wealth. It is not your truth, and everything you do is then built upon a lie-support system. Even though you might receive a note for currency, whether it be a dollar bill or a check, there is not a surplus for exchange. There is only enough to exchange for basic living.

Many people in America work very hard, but that work energy is being invested into someone else's idea and truth instead of their own. As a result, they might have some dollar bills, but they surely don't have money and are definitely not on the trajectory for true wealth. You have to consider where your energy is spent, or where the work that you do is done. The only path to the highest frequency of abundance is the path that follows your own truth, as defined by your ideas.

Truth = Ideas

Most people have great ideas, but those ideas die, generally because the necessary energy to bring those ideas to accomplishment are diverted toward bringing someone else's idea to accomplishment. Don't get me wrong—there's nothing wrong with making a living. But rest assured that you're not building wealth at the same time. Here's a great way to explain this dynamic.

I'm going to go to the top of the food chain of what you think money is to prove my point. A football player or basketball player signs a contract for $15 million to play over a certain amount of time. It's the biggest sum of money he has ever seen, let alone received, in his lifetime. He immediately goes out and buys homes and cars valued at, let's say, $35 million, which are owned by the NFL and NBA corporations. He plays his sport, receiving legal tender, whether it be cash or check, and then gives it back to the NFL or NBA when he pays for the house and cars. The player is actually playing at a net loss of $20 million. They might be holding $15 million in their hand, but it's not money because they have to pay back $35 million.

This is also classic in the music industry and in Hollywood. You see the superstars living in big mansions and driving big cars that don't belong to them. They are singing and entertaining under someone else's ownership. Even though they appear rich, they are living under the frequency of a lower echelon of financial existence. What happens to the stars when they retire? You generally find them right back where they started. They are not experiencing true wealth, but the illusion of wealth. They are not living within or establishing a life-support system, but a lie-support system.

You must evaluate what system you live under. There's nothing wrong with having no money, but I don't want you to fool yourself into thinking that you do have money or wealth if you're actually living under the frequency of lower financial mediums of exchange.

The 8 Laws of Experience

To keep from falling into the lower frequency of medium exchange—the lie-support system—you must master the art of taking an idea from your head, putting in the energy to advance that idea, and moving the idea from an idea to an experience. Here are the eight laws of experience developed by a close friend of mine to help you do just that. These laws of experience will help you stay in the creative and innovative mode of personal development, which will reflect into your financial experiences.

The 8 Laws of Experience are:
1. Exploration
2. Expenditure
3. Expectation
4. Expertise

5. Exposure
6. Expression
7. Expansion
8. Exportation

1. Exploration: Create New Ideas

Exploration is a state of existence. Do not be afraid to try new things. Do not be afraid to try what you think. Place a value on what you think and stay ahead of the game. You can't explore what is or what already exists, because the next best thing is beyond that. The best space for exploration is within your own mind. Move beyond traditional thinking and into innovation.

2. Expenditure: Do Not Be Left with Less

Decide who and what you will exchange with. The only way to have true financial greatness is to base your exchanges on the ideas that have been formulated within your spirit, which is your truth. Only your own truth can build true wealth. Stay firm on the terms of your exchanges. This is the basis of true relationships, as all relationships should lead to more. As you participate in exchanges, take a measurement of what you have in the end and adjust as necessary.

3. Expectation: Decide into by Tying In

You must decide what to tie your mind to. Once you have created an idea, and subsequently created the relationships around the idea, you must set expectations for manifestation. Be careful of being distracted. When your mind is turned to other interests, you will lose the energy of expectation towards what you desire. Tie into your expectations only. This is the only way to create the energy necessary to manifest what you want because your work or actions will follow your energy.

4. Expertise: Knowledge Forces Ability

This is what you decide to know. If you're not afraid of your ideas, your body will create the information for the formulation of your ideas. You have an incredible physiological system that is designed to push what's on your mind into being. Not only can you facilitate the idea, but you can formulate the information and the education to bring the idea into an experience. You have to trust this process and understand that the easiest thing for you to produce is your own truth. If you have to educate yourself to become an expert towards your own truth, do so.

5. Exposure: Habitats/Sense of Place

Habits stem from what you expose yourself to based on your expectation. You become the people with whom you spend your time. Their energy becomes your energy. You must make sure the energies that are in proximity to you serve your best interest. Habits become a place of comfort. Make sure that you're in an environment that invests the habitual energy that is in alignment with what you want.

6. Expression: Highest Behavior Within, No Less

Expression is how you show up in the world, which is based on your energetic imprint. The question is, what are you doing every day that's related to what you want? Everything that you do must have something to do with the idea in your head. Remember, it is your ideas that are the basis and the definition of what money is, especially when you move that idea to physiological existence. This becomes your medium of exchange. So, you must put in the work, the energy, and the activity towards the discoveries within your explorations.

7. Expansion: Significance = Sign + Evidence

What you expand out of your idea is the evidence of your exchanges. It is your exchanges that cause expansion. You cannot grow and transform without the beneficial exchanges that come from others. Just like the universe, you are in a continuous state of expansion, and if you're not expanding, you are dying. It is your expansion and your personal growth that gives you significance, or as I call it sign-evidence.

8. Exportation: Access to New Levels, Access Up

Now you must take the first seven laws of experience and move them to an even higher frequency. Keep repeating this process and watch your ideas transform into greatness. Not only will you see the transformations, you'll experience the frequency of the greatest finance and wealth. Practicing these principles will allow you to raise the frequency of your personal experiences from primal existences to creative and innovative existences. It is on that level of energy or frequency where true wealth exists.

CHAPTER THIRTEEN
Conclusion

The five frequencies of your life—spiritual, mindset, physical, relationships, and financial—are not new, as they have been moving throughout your life your entire existence. Now that you understand the mechanics and the importance of each of them, you have the power to move *them*. You are equipped to strategically and intentionally manipulate your personal frequencies to ensure you are always playing on the highest frequencies possible. As you align these truths in your life, you will be the master of your destiny—the conscious creator of your experiences and outcomes. All that you most desire is accessible to you. You simply have to identify the frequency on which it rests, and then dial in.

Consider this country's rich history of achievers: Colonel Sanders, whose chicken recipe was rejected by 1,008 people before he got his break, and whose restaurants are now found all over the world. Thomas Edison, who failed ten thousand times trying to discover the secret to the light bulb, and twenty thousand times while inventing the phonograph. Helen Keller, who was deaf and blind, yet who became an inspiration to the nation. Ray Charles and Stevie Wonder, both of whom have had massive success in the music industry, despite their blindness. These are all people who had limited resources and had every reason to be down and out. And yet, they lived their lives to the fullest—in a way where they just couldn't wait to wake up in the morning and see what tomorrow had to offer because they had something to bring into that day.

Conclusion

When you hear the stories of other people who have been through hard times, you realize that if they have done it, you can do it, too. You realize that you don't have to hide in the depths of the darkness of your story. Listen to these stories, and then build your story along the way.

I am here to give you hope and to show you how the stories that you have will empower the power within you. There is strength in your stories. Your life has significance because you are here to help other people. However, you can only help them through the pain and the experiences that you have gone through. It wasn't so bad after all because it has a meaning, and it is a meaning that you can't buy with all the gold in the world. You can't buy it with millions of dollars. These are gifts that only come by living. When you move through it, you see the contrast of the universe. You come to understand possibilities because you lived the lack, just like you understand hot because you've experienced cold, positive because of negative, and good times because you have had bad times. If you have never had a bad time, how can you really appreciate the good? Life is going to happen to you, but it is going to make you better. All things work together for your good.

Even mistakes and failures can help you to succeed in the right situations. The trick is to intentionally use them for your good. Do not go into the blame game or ask, "Why is this happening to me?" Instead, step into a state of still meditation so that you can be an observer. Ask, "What am I supposed to learn from this? How can I grow from this?" Learn to ask yourself better questions in order to get better answers and outcomes. When you change the way you look at things, the things you look at will *always* change.

Whatever you have been through, that does not define who you are, and it is not your identity. Those were just situations. Learn from them and own them, but never let them own you. If you are feeling trapped in the frequency of old stories, know that you can create a new reality at any time. A new frequency is waiting for you.

It is there, in the room with you right now. It is already residing in you. It is just waiting for you to say, "Yes,"—to make a decision to go forth into it, and to stay there.

Once you do, the laws of attraction kick in and you have the advantage of the law of vibration—that vibration, that frequency, and that energy, which is always moving and seeking a receptor, just as radio waves are always there and always seeking the radio receptor. However, you have to turn it on in order to access those waves. When you do, and if you tune in to the right station, you are going to access that specific frequency you're looking for.

Remember, you can only tune in to one station at a time. Once you tap in to that high frequency, do not go back to lower frequencies. Do not let fear cause you to dial backwards. That will happen if you feel like you are not worthy of the place you are stepping in to. However, if you live in the imagined fairytale land of expectancy, daring to declare, "My life has meaning. I can do something greater than I have ever dreamed. There is more for me." Then that declaration will spawn a belief, and that belief will keep you tuned in to that higher frequency until you know without a doubt that you belong there—and that it belongs in you. The heart of this truth resides in every person that breaths. Every human being knows in their spirit there is more, but they don't know how to tap in to it. You have to find the light-bearers who can show you the way.

Get a Coach

None of us can reach our fullest potential by ourselves. Just as I have worked with a personal trainer to improve my physical frequency, I have learned to get a trainer and a mentor in every aspect of my life. Find the people who have arrived at your desired location, and let them map out the way for you to get there, too. You do not have to reinvent the wheel. Just because you are taking the first step does not mean there is no path. In fact, there are those who have built paved, four-lane highways. Don't go hacking through the brush when you can take the expressway.

That's why I always try to make sure I surround myself with those who are part of my vision and harmony. It is important to align yourself with and be in the service of people who are playing at the highest level possible. When I enroll with other people and I am part of their vision and harmony, and they are part of mine, we experience the truth that light attracts light. Often, people ask the question, "How can I find these people? I am not good enough to be there. I don't have their resources." Service is the doorway to get there. Good people are always looking for good people.

Letting Go

In order to move into the frequency of light, you have got to be able to let go of the people and things in your life that are not in harmony with that light. I know from experience that this is the most difficult part of transforming. You don't want to let go of friends, or let go of the addictions and numbing practices that have taken the edge off of the pain that comes from living at a low frequency. However, you cannot experience the rewards that come from moving into a heightened space without first releasing the weights that are holding you down. It would be nice if it could be the other way around—if you could have the reward before you make the sacrifice. But life is not this way. All you can do in order to get a glimpse of that promise is to look at the lives of those who are already living in that space of higher frequency. Observe the people who are already living the life you dream of. That is the shadow of what is to come as you courageously release your hold on your attachments.

The truth is that when you are striving to move to another frequency, your attachments will separate themselves from you anyway because they cannot survive where you are going. To an AM station, FM does not exist. You only see what you are tapped in to. This means that you don't actually even have to cut anyone off. You just have to cut you on. When you turn yourself on, life turns in your favor. The things that you want start showing up. Your team and family will get better as you get better. More money will come to you because you are living in an abundant mindset. You will be able to live higher because you are thinking higher. You will experience and receive more because you are more.

You can be sure that letting go does not in any way imply that you will be alone or abandoning people you love. When you tap in to a higher frequency, you are then able to lead other people out of the lower frequencies in which they live. People will follow you. They will roll with you and listen to you as long as they feel like you can give them an experience they can't find anywhere else. Are you going to be the person who's going to give an experience, or are you going to be part of someone else's experience? Are you going to set the tone of the experience and the frequency of the energy you walk into, or are you going to become a part of the energy that's already there? Are you going to become a difference maker, or are you going to disappear into a sea of people all flowing downstream?

It is in your design to be different. Your DNA, your pupils, your fingerprints, and your cellular makeup are unique in all the world. No two people are alike, but we tend to want to get together and be alike. This is unnatural because it is not natural for you to be like anyone else. It is natural for you to strive to the heavens to be the best you can be and to challenge your mind. Bruce Lee, one of my childhood heroes, said, "The usefulness of a cup is in its emptiness." You become empty as you position yourself to receive knowledge. In order to reach a higher state, you must learn how to get there. Education is key because it gives you a new reference point. Otherwise, you will have no reference to know when you have arrived—or when it's time to keep walking.

Write Your Future

It is your responsibility to step into this space of a higher frequency, and yours alone. Sometimes it is a lonely road, but you have got to do it. You will find your reward at the end of the journey, and you don't know what twists and turns the journey is going to take. It may not happen on the first step or the thousandth step, but when you get there, you will know that you have arrived—even if you don't know until the very moment that you turn the corner.

You have to be like the person with the axe who is trying to knock down the mighty oak tree. You have to understand that one whack with the axe is not going to make the tree fall. Nor will it fall on the second whack or the third. However, if you continue to hit the tree with your axe, eventually the tree will fall. In the meantime, you get into a rhythm and a flow of a new frequency—the frequency of growth. You feel your muscles building and your mind beginning to focus. Whack, whack, whack. It becomes a beat that forms a new song. You will fall in love with that song and cherish the power in the journey. It will be the fuel that drives you forward.

Will you be perfect? No. Absolutely not. But don't beat yourself up. Just get better and grow. Don't bail and don't let anybody compromise the love you have for humanity. As you continue to live this way and begin to build muscle, you get stronger and stronger until one day, you are the person you meant to be, living the life you meant to live, and receiving all that you set out to receive and to achieve. Keep going. Never give up. How do you eat an elephant? One bite at a time. By the yard is hard, but inch by inch, everything is a cinch. You don't have to hit the finish line right now. Just commit to do the workout today.

You can tell your future if you are willing to write.

Now, let the writing begin!

About the Author

James Dentley is an entrepreneur, best-selling author, philanthropist, and one of the nation's top Life and Business Strategists. As one of the world's most renowned motivational speakers, James Dentley is a dynamic personality and highly sought after resource in business and professional circles for Fortune 500 CEOs, small business owners, non-profits, and community leaders from all sectors of society looking to expand opportunity.

James Dentley is the best-selling author of the books 'The Frequencies of Top Performers' and 'MLM Mastery,' and he created the #1 speakers' and communication program 'Inspired2Speak: Action Camp.' His passion is to empower entrepreneurs and business owners to create massive success and to achieve their dreams. James' passion for coaching and mentoring speakers has transformed "good speakers to great speakers and great speakers to legendary." He has spent over three decades working with start-ups to major global brands to help them increase sales, productivity, and overall success. He is an innovator with a remarkable ability to determine and build success plans to help business owners seize immediate market opportunities. For everyone that owns a business or

would like to capitalize on their entrepreneurial dream, his message will enlighten with knowledge and action principles to turn that passion into success!

In his mission to continually impact the lives of millions all over the world, Dentley has made headlines by partnering and lending his voice to disruptive companies in the financial services arena. Addressing audiences from North, South, and Latin America, Europe, Asia-Pacific and his most recent tour including London, Thailand, Germany, Dubai, Caribbean just to name a few, James Dentley is invited back again and again for his powerful message and the ability to connect deeply with people from all walks of life. It isn't just his great smile, humble nature, and his way with words that motivates people to take action like never before; when people face roadblocks or adversity, it is the depth of his knowledge on achievement that creates lasting results.

James Dentley is a gentle giant that teaches straight-from-the-heart, passion and high-energy, motivates audiences to step beyond their limitations and into their greatness in many ways. Over the past two decades, James has expanded his role from keynote speaker to Master Speaker and Master Storyteller, creating the kind of workshop learning experience that got him committed to personal-and-professional development many years earlier. His charisma, warmth, and humor have transformed ordinary people into extraordinary achievers by using his own life, and his in-depth study of others' challenges, to build an understanding of what works, what doesn't work, and why.

As a philanthropist and revered role-model by his colleagues, Dentley received an iconic award from 'U4G (Unite4: Good)', and The City Gala, both organizations dedicated to building a sustainable social good movement. It's James' personal goal to get people around the world active in spreading good by partnering with U4G. James has funded numerous programs and most recently 'The Doty Foundation: Georgia Doty HIV & Hepatitis Community Outreach

Inc. Hepatitis, HCDC, and 'A Safe Haven' offering children of the south side of Chicago.

James Dentley is committed to motivating and training today's generation to be achievers and leaders as he introduces new audiences every day to "If I fall, I will get up. If I am beaten, I will return. I will never stop getting better, never." and "This is why I live my dreams." James Dentley's audio series, 'Mentor to Millions' and 'Interview with the Masters', remains his all-time bestseller for its acclaimed impact worldwide.

In 2010, he formed his company, NBC University to spread his message to a wider audience. NBC University provides success education programs around the world. The programs are designed for individuals, companies, and organizations that are interested in creating even more success. James is committed to raising the awareness of entrepreneurs, business owners, and organizations worldwide! The unique programs offered through NBC University are designed to assist entrepreneurs in creating the focus, plans, and partnerships required to build multi-million dollar companies!

James has an extensive background in network marketing, real estate investing and building businesses all over the world. Over the past two decades, his firm has specialized in helping companies launch, grow, and create exponential value in the market. The 'Inspired2speak' and Limitless programs offered through NBC University are designed to help entrepreneurs create the focus, plans, and partnerships required to build multi-million dollar companies.

In business as in real life, there are always going to be ups and downs. However, where there is a will, there is always a way to achieve amazing results for your organization when James Dentley fills the room with his high-impact, customized message and standing ovation performance!